MAXIMIZE YOUR READING

1

Maximize Your Reading 1

Pearson Education, Inc., 221 River Street, Hoboken, NJ 07030 USA

Staff credits: The people who made up the **Maximize Your Reading** team are Pietro Alongi, Rhea Banker, Tracey Munz Cataldo, Mindy DePalma, Gina DiLillo, Niki Lee, Amy McCormick, Lindsay Richman, and Paula Van Ells.

Text composition: MPS North America LLC

Design: EMC Design Ltd

Photo credits: Cover: Moodboard/Getty Images. Page 1: Pressmaster/Fotolia; 2 (left): Absolut/Fotolia; 2 (right): Antiksu/Fotolia; 8 (bottom): Monkey Business/Fotolia; 8 (top): Oksana Perkins/Fotolia; 9 (bottom): Bst2012/Fotolia; 9 (top): Herby (Herbert) Me/Fotolia; 10 (bottom): Vlad_g/Fotolia; 10 (top): Luliia Sokolovska/Fotolia; 11 (bottom): Africa Studio/Fotolia; 11 (top): Kathrin39/Fotolia; 15 (bottom, left): Sergii Mostovyi/Fotolia; 15 (bottom, right): Galyna Andrushko/Fotolia; 15 (center, right): Kzenon/Fotolia; 15 (top): Serghei Velusceac/Fotolia; 16: Beboy/Fotolia; 17: Kate Shephard/Fotolia; 18: Jurra8/Fotolia; 19 (bottom): Vibe Images/Fotolia; 19 (center, left): Auremar/Fotolia; 19 (center, right): Jan S./Fotolia; 19 (top): Michael Jung/Fotolia; 20: Benjamin Simeneta/Fotolia; 55 (left): Monkey Business/Fotolia; 55 (right): Gina Smith/Fotolia; 56 (bottom, left): Avava/Fotolia; 56 (bottom, right): Lurii Sokolov/Fotolia; 56 (top, left): Bst2012/Fotolia; 56 (top, right): : Pressmaster/Fotolia; 67 (bottom): Dušan Zidar/Fotolia; 67 (top): WavebreakmediaMicro/Fotolia; 75 (bottom): Ilike/Fotolia; 75 (top): Alphaspirit/Fotolia; 151: Sonya Etchison/Fotolia; 152 (bottom, right): Roman Pyshchyk/Fotolia; 152 (top): Tyler Olson/Fotolia.

ISBN-13: 978-0-13-466139-1   ISBN-10: 0-13-466139-7

Printed in the United States of America

2   16

pearsonelt.com/maximizeyourreading

CONTENTS

Reading Level 1 – Beginner

PRE-TEST

Part 1   Comprehension Skills

Circle the letter of the correct answer.

1 The article above is about _____ .

   a students getting new books at school

   b schools that don't have money for technology

   c students who don't like new technology

   d students using new technology at school

2 The article on p. 1 is about _____ .
  a the importance of sleep
  b how sleep is not good for your health
  c how a lot of sleep is not good
  d the usefulness of naps

3 This book is about _____ .
  a how new dogs are better than old dogs
  b how dogs can do magic tricks
  c how to train your dog
  d how to care for old dogs

4 This book is about _____ .
  a ideas for traveling
  b backpacks
  c trains
  d tipping in restaurants

Part 2 Comprehension Skills

Read the list. Check (✓) the topic of the list.

The topic is:

__ classroom

__ computer

__ desk

__ whiteboard

__ pencil

__ book

__ chair

__ teacher

Part 3   Comprehension Skills

Read the paragraph. Circle the letter of the correct answer.

My school has many clubs after school. There is a game club on Monday. My friend and I go to that one. You play all kinds of games with your friends. On Wednesday, there are two clubs. One is soccer club, and one is book club. I go to soccer club, and my brother goes to book club. On Friday, there is exercise club. The students run and exercise in that club. There is something for everyone!

1 The topic of this paragraph is _____ .
  a soccer
  b after school
  c clubs
  d games

Are you a happy person? There are many reasons it is good to be happy. For example, doctors say that happy people live long lives because they do not have stress. Another reason is that they see a problem and believe they can overcome it. In addition, happy people have a lot of friends. People want to be around happy people.

2 The topic of this paragraph is _____ .
  a making friends
  b overcoming problems
  c the benefits of being happy
  d going to the doctor

There are many places to live downtown, but the new apartment building on Main Street is very popular. Many young people live there. It has a gym and a lounge. Many people go to the gym after work to exercise. Then, after they exercise, they go to the lounge to relax and meet friends. The building also has a coffee shop and two restaurants. Many young people go out to dinner often, and these restaurants are very convenient for them.

3 The topic of this paragraph is _____ .
  a a new apartment building
  b young people
  c new restaurants
  d exercising and relaxing

Part 4   Comprehension Skills

Read the paragraph. Determine the order of each event. Then number the sentences in the correct order.

Next week, some international students will visit our school. First, the director of the school will greet the students in the main lobby. Next, the director will take them on a tour of the school. They will see the classrooms and meet some of the teachers and students. Then they will walk to the gymnasium and watch the dance performance our students planned. After that, they will eat lunch in the cafeteria. Some American students will sit with the international students during lunch. Finally, the international students will begin their classes.

___ The students will get a tour of the school.

___ Some international students will visit our school.

___ The students will see the classrooms and meet some teachers.

___ The students will begin classes.

___ The students will watch a dance performance.

___ The director will greet the students.

___ The students will eat lunch.

Part 5   Comprehension Skills

Read the paragraph. How many examples related to the main idea are there? Circle the correct number of examples in the paragraph.

Are you a happy person? There are many reasons it is good to be happy. For example, doctors say that happy people live long lives because they do not have stress. Another reason is that they see a problem and believe they can overcome it. In addition, happy people have a lot of friends. People want to be around happy people.

2

3

4

5

Part 6   Comprehension Skills

Read the paragraph. Underline the sentences that have a sequence key word.

Last year, I went to a party at my friend's house. I met a man named Louis there. As soon as I met him, I knew he was different from other people I knew. We talked and danced all night. The next day, he called me, and we went for a walk in the park. It is easy to talk to him. We have so many things in common. After a few more months, we got married! Now, we are living happily!

Part 7   Comprehension Skills

Read the text below. Circle the letter of the correct answer of each question on the next page.

A: Slow down!

B: I am going the speed limit for this road.

A: Watch out for that car!

B: I see it. Please don't yell. I can't concentrate on driving!

A: Sorry. I am just a little nervous.

1 Where are these people?

    a They are at work.

    b They are in a car.

    c They are on bicycles.

    d They are on a train.

My family moved from China to Chicago when I was seven years old. That was both good and bad. I learned new things, but I moved away from all of my friends. When I first got to Chicago, everything was so different. The people, the language, and the food were all very different from China. I didn't know how to speak English very well, either. It was difficult. Now, I am ten years old and living happily in Chicago. I still miss my friends and China, but we go back to visit every year. I have lots of new friends now, and it's great to know two different cultures and ways of life.

2 What were the good and bad parts about moving?

    a The bad part was that he had to move. The good part was that he moved to Chicago.

    b The good part was that he learned new things. The bad part was that he missed his friends.

    c The good part was that he moved to Chicago. The bad part was that he was seven years old.

    d The bad part was that he moved to Chicago. The good part was that he loved China.

Part 8 Vocabulary Building

Read the dictionary entry. Classify the underlined parts. Circle the letters of the two correct answers.

masculine /ˈmaskyələn/ *adjective*, 1) having qualities that are considered to be typical of men

    a pronunciation

    b part of speech

    c meaning of word

    d entry word

Part 9 Vocabulary Building

Look at the list of words. Circle the correct prefix and its meaning.

discount, disconnect, discharge, discourage

Prefix: dis, un, mis, pre, under, re, non

Meaning: not, under, wrong, before, again

Part 10   Vocabulary Building

Circle the letter of the correct answer.

Which suffix can be added to the root word *color*?

a er   **b** al   **c** ness   **d** ful

Part 11   Vocabulary Building

Draw lines to match the words with the correct parts of speech.

1 sad   adverb

2 sadness   noun

3 sadly   adjective

Part 12   Vocabulary Building

Read the sentences. Circle the word that explains the underlined word.

This tree is on top of my bicycle. Can you help me <u>hoist</u> it? We need to lift it off my bike quickly.

Part 13   Vocabulary Building

Read the sentences. What part of speech is the missing word? Circle the letter of the correct answer.

The test was long and _____ . I didn't know half of the problems.

a verb   **b** noun   **c** adjective   **d** adverb

Part 14   Vocabulary Building

Read the sentences. What is the general meaning of the underlined word? Circle the letter of the correct answer.

My dad is always an <u>optimist</u>. He always believes that good things will happen.

a good things

b someone who believes things will end well

c someone who believes things will end poorly

d a good father

Part 15   Vocabulary Building

Circle the letter of the phrase that correctly completes the sentence.

Please remember to _____ the lights when you leave tonight.

a turn off   **b** turn up   **c** turn in

Part 16   Thinking in English

Write the phrase that correctly completes the sentence.

| have a party | take a shower | sit down |
| write it down | wait for me | |

1 I am so tired. My feet are hurting. Is there a place for me to _____ ?

2 After you get to the mall, please _____ . I want to go in with you.

3 I can never remember your address. Can you _____ please? Here is some paper and a pencil.

4 Tomorrow is Joe's birthday. We will _____ for him after school. We're going to have cake and ice cream.

5 Janet likes to _____ in the morning. The water wakes her up.

Part 17   Thinking in English

Read the sentence. Circle the letter of the best meaning for the underlined word.

1 My family <u>moved</u> from China to Chicago.
  a changed from one position to another
  b changed one's home from one place to another
  c went very fast
  d visited

2 It's great to know two different <u>cultures</u> and ways of life.
  a countries from around the world
  b arts, beliefs, and behaviors of a group of people
  c people from another country
  d languages

3 I still <u>miss</u> my friends.
  a feel sad because you can't be with someone
  b not go somewhere or do something
  c not see or hear something
  d not hit or catch something

4 We <u>go back</u> to visit every year.
  a travel
  b give
  c return
  d call

COMPREHENSION SKILLS

Previewing and Predicting

PREVIEWING

> **Presentation**
>
> **Previewing Using Visuals**
> Before you read, look at the pictures. The pictures give you information about the text. This information can help you understand the text.

Practice 1

Look at the picture from the newspaper article. What is the topic of the article? Circle the letter of the correct answer.

1 The article above is about _____ .
  a a bridge that needs repairs after storms
  b famous bridges across the United States
  c students learning how to build a bridge

2 The article above is about _____ .
  a a celebration for firefighters
  b a firefighter saving a woman in a car
  c a woman becoming a firefighter

3 The article above is about _____ .

  a children helping disabled dogs

  b children teaching dogs some tricks

  c dogs helping disabled children

4 The article above is about _____ .

  a a girl getting injured at a swim competition

  b a girl losing a race

  c a girl winning a medal in swimming

Practice 2

Look at the picture on the page. What is the topic of the book? Circle the letter of the correct answer.

1 The book above is about _____ .

    a hiking in the mountains

    b a family taking a trip

    c camping along the Pacific Ocean

2 The book above is about _____ .

    a a boy getting lost in a hot air balloon

    b a man saving a woman in a tree with his hot air balloon

    c hot air balloons

3 The book above is about _____ .

   a a boy and his horse

   b a girl and her horse

   c a girl and her pet dog

4 The book above is about _____ .

   a a girl who makes dresses

   b learning how to sew on a sewing machine

   c learning how to type on the computer

Previewing Using Bold Text and Headings

To preview a text, look at the title, subtitle, and words in bold print or italics. These headings give you clues about the information in the text.

Practice 3

Read the title, subtitle, and heading of the newspaper article. Circle the letter of the topic of the paragraph.

1 **a** This was the first time the man played the lottery.
   b The man plays the lottery every day.
   c The man doesn't have a job.
   d The man doesn't like the lottery.
   e This was the first time the man lost his job.

2 **a** The man is rich now.
   b The man had a hard life.
   c It is hard to win the lottery.
   d It is hard to buy a lottery ticket.
   e Life is hard.

3 **a** The man can't find his leg.
   b The man doesn't like to work.
   c There was an accident at work, and the man's leg was cut off.
   d The man is lazy.
   e The man has a good job.

4 **a** The man is getting married.
   b The man is getting an artificial life.
   c The man is going to play the lottery every day.
   d The man is getting an artificial leg.
   e The man is getting a new house.

Practice 4

Read the title of the chapter and the section heading. Circle the letter of the correct answer.

1 The section above is about _____ .
  a a shark attack
  b sea mammals
  c types of fish
  d various types of sharks

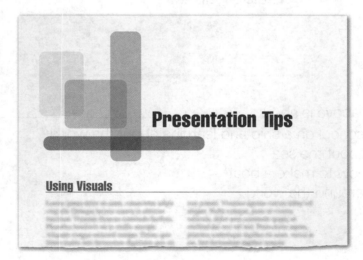

2 The section above is about _____ .
  a making eye contact
  b making visuals for your presentation
  c using visuals in your presentation
  d visualizing your audience

Dangerous Jobs

Deep Sea Fishing

3 The section above is about _____ .
   a fishing for fun
   b fishing in the deep water of the ocean
   c lake fishing
   d sailing on the deep sea

Special Schools

A School on the Seas

4 The section above is about _____ .
   a going to school on a ship and learning about the world
   b learning about the sea
   c learning how to make a boat
   d traveling around the world

PREDICTING

Presentation

Predicting

Look at the title and visuals before reading a text. They often tell you the most important ideas in a text. Then predict or guess what the author of the text might say about these ideas. Making predictions helps you get ready to read.

Practice 1

Look at the cover and read the title of the book. Circle the letter of the correct answer.

1 This book is about _____ .
  a how a caterpillar becomes a butterfly
  b how to care for a butterfly
  c types of butterflies

2 This book is about _____ .
  a a girl and her dog
  b a girl and her horse
  c two horses

3 This book is about _____ .
  a a boy who likes to paint
  b an art teacher
  c learning how to paint

4 This book is about _____ .
  a a climber's trip to the top of Mt. Everest
  b historic climbs of Mt. Everest
  c how to climb Mt. Everest

1

2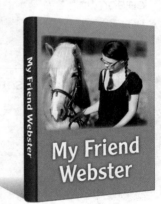

3

4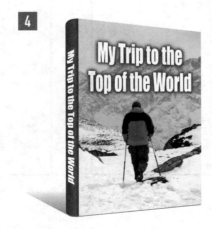

Practice 2

Look at the picture and read the title of the book. What do you think the book is about? Write each description in the correct boxes.

1

activities for celebrating the holiday	history of the holiday flowers	date of the holiday cutting down trees	description of the holiday tree diseases

Ideas in the book	Ideas not in the book

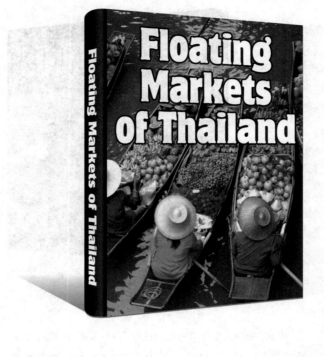

2

| location of floating markets | floating markets around the world | recipes for Thai food | things sold at floating markets |
| people of Thailand | places to visit in Thailand | how to get to floating markets | description of floating markets |

Information in the book	Information not in the book

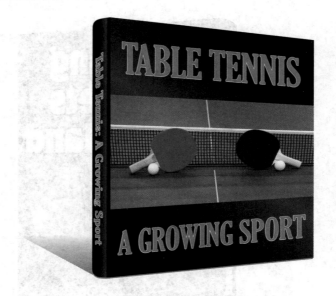

3

| a schedule of table tennis events around the world | a story about a girl who has a magic table tennis table | rules of the sport where to buy a table tennis ball |
| history of table tennis | countries where table tennis is played | |

Ideas in the book	Ideas not in the book

Practice 3

Look at the picture and read the title of the article. What information do you think is mentioned in the article? Circle the letters of all of the correct answers.

Dog Saves Family in Fire

1 The article above has information about _____ .

   a a dog that wakes up a family

   b a dog that takes a walk

   c a dog that likes to swim

   d a dog that smells fire

   e a family that gets out of their house safely

   f a family that doesn't like dogs

Senior Citizens Make Old Park New Again

2 The article above has information about _____ .

   a elderly people getting hurt at a park

   b elderly people destroying a park

   c elderly people cleaning up a park

   d elderly people making an old park beautiful

   e a park that was dirty and old

   f elderly people building a new park

Tornado Destroys Neighborhood

3 The article above has information about _____ .

    a the date of the tornado

    b how tornados form

    c how to prepare for a tornado

    d areas of the neighborhood that were destroyed

    e where to go if a tornado comes

    f the number of houses destroyed

    g how to help people affected by the tornado

Identifying Topics and Main Ideas

IDENTIFYING THE TOPIC OF A LIST

> **Presentation**
>
> Identifying the Topic of a List
> Look at the words in the list. What do the words have in common? The topic of the list is what they all have in common.

Practice 1

Read the list of words. Circle the letter of the word in each list that names the topic of the list.

Example:

1 a doctors
   b teachers
   c occupations
   d lawyers

2 a living rooms
   b kitchens
   c bedrooms
   d attics
   e bathrooms
   f rooms

3 a vehicles
   b cars
   c bicycles
   d buses
   e trucks
   f trains

4 a hotels
   b banks
   c buildings
   d schools
   e bus stations
   f hospitals

5 a title
   b pages
   c cover
   d book parts
   e table of contents
   f appendix

Practice 2

Read the list of words. Circle the word that names the topic of the list.

1 family, wife, sister, father, niece, cousin
2 desk, classroom, whiteboard, computer, chair, teacher, student
3 monitor, keyboard, computer, hard drive, mouse, software, printer
4 tree, grass, river, nature, mountain, forest
5 soccer, football, tennis, basketball, sport, golf
6 wedding, birthday party, celebration, graduation, farewell party, welcome party

Practice 3

Match a word list to a topic. Draw a line to make each match.

1 breakfast, dinner, lunch, brunch, supper   meal

2 math, English, science, physics, geography, history   money

3 fever, sore throat, headache, backache, earache   symptom

4 dollar, yen, euro, pound, peso, franc   country

5 soda, coffee, tea, water, wine, juice   drink

6 Mexico, Japan, China, Canada, Germany, Brazil   subject

UNDERSTANDING PARAGRAPHS

Understanding Paragraphs

A paragraph is a group of sentences about the same topic. The beginning of a paragraph has a sentence that states the topic. This is the topic sentence. The other sentences in a paragraph relate to the topic sentence.

Practice 1

Read the passage. Is it a paragraph or just a collection of sentences? Circle the letter of the correct answer.

Every Saturday, my husband does the same thing. He wakes up at 7:30 A.M. and reads the newspaper. He then gets dressed and works in the yard. Yard work is good exercise. Exercise is important for your health. Eating lots of fruits and vegetables is good for your health.

1 This is _____ .

   a a paragraph
   b not a paragraph

We all know that classical music helps relax your body and mind, but many researchers agree that classical music also makes you smarter. There is something about the music that helps the brain focus. Many studies show that people are able to do mental tasks better and faster after listening to classical music than they were able to before. This idea is called the "Mozart Effect."

2 This is _____ .

   a a paragraph
   b not a paragraph

One of the most amazing natural places in the world is the Grand Canyon. It is located in the state of Arizona, and many visitors go there each year to see natural beauty. Arizona is a dry state. The Yuma Desert is in Arizona. Many kinds of cacti and lizards live in the desert.

3 This is _____ .

    a a paragraph

    b not a paragraph

My family goes on a summer vacation every year. Last summer, we went camping at a nearby lake. We brought our boat with us, and we relaxed and swam in the lake every day. Every night, we had a big campfire. We roasted hot dogs and marshmallows over the fire and sang songs. We had a great time.

4 This is _____ .

    a a paragraph

    b not a paragraph

It's important to have good study habits at home. There are many distractions at home, and it can be hard to study there. Study in an area without a television or radio. Television and radio can be very distracting. Also, turn off your phone when you study. A phone call can distract you from your studies.

5 This is _____ .

    a a paragraph

    b not a paragraph

Practice 2

Read the passages. The last passage is on the next page. Circle the letter of the passage that is a paragraph.

a Are you tired of going to the same place for vacation? Why not try someplace new and interesting? An ice hotel is a different place to go. An ice hotel is a hotel made from ice and snow!

b There are a few ice hotels around the world. The most famous ones are in Finland and Sweden. The people of Finland speak Finnish. Finland is next to Sweden. Sweden and Finland border the Baltic Sea. Commercial fishing is a popular job in Sweden.

c When you check into an ice hotel, you check in at the warm part of the hotel. Then you get into your warm clothes and go to the actual ice hotel. Your room has a bed made from ice. On top of the bed are warm blankets so you stay warm at night.

d After you arrive, you go to the restaurant for dinner. The benches around the tables are heated, but everything else is made out of ice. The food is prepared at the hotel and is delicious. There are many kinds of special foods, including caviar and fresh sushi.

e You can stay as many nights as you like in the warm part of the hotel, but it is recommended to stay only one night in the ice hotel. There are other things to do in the other parts of the hotel. It is important to stay warm in cold weather. You can get frostbite if you don't wear gloves and a hat in winter.

IDENTIFYING THE TOPIC OF A PARAGRAPH

> **Presentation**
>
> **Identifying the Topic of a Paragraph**
> The topic of a paragraph is what the paragraph is about. One way to find the topic of a paragraph is to look for a word or phrase that is repeated often in the sentences. That word or phrase is the topic.

Practice 1

Read the paragraph. Circle the letter of the correct answer.

My favorite sport is lacrosse. Lacrosse is a team sport and was originally a Native American game. It is played with a stick and a ball. The stick has a net on it that is designed to catch and hold the lacrosse ball. Lacrosse is very popular in Canada and the United States.

1 The topic of this paragraph is _____ .
   a Canada
   b team sports
   c Native Americans
   d lacrosse

I love my garden. It is full of beautiful flowers and trees. My husband and I planted the garden a few years ago. It's my favorite place to go. I go there to read and relax. We also have dinner parties in the garden. It is my very special place.

2 The topic of this paragraph is _____ .
   a flowers
   b trees
   c a garden
   d the author's husband

Many people practice martial arts. Karate, taekwondo, and judo are all forms of martial arts. People practice martial arts for various reasons. Exercise, self-defense, self-control, and competition are all reasons that people practice martial arts. Martial arts are originally from Asia, but they are popular around the world.

3 The topic of this paragraph is _____ .
   a karate
   b martial arts
   c exercise
   d art

We know little about Cleopatra. She was born in 69 BCE, in Alexandria, Egypt. Cleopatra was the last pharaoh, or ruler, of Egypt. Rome took control of Egypt after Cleopatra's death. People believe that Cleopatra killed herself after the death of her husband, Marc Antony.

4 The topic of this paragraph is _____ .
   a Marc Antony
   b Egypt
   c pharaohs
   d Cleopatra

Practice 2

Read the paragraph. Circle the letter of the correct answer.

My great-grandparents were born in Germany. After they got married, they came to the United States in 1882. They wanted a better life. My great-grandfather worked as a baker, and my great-grandmother made dresses. They worked very hard and saved their money. They liked their new life in the United States.

1 The topic of this paragraph is _____ .
   a the United States
   b bakers
   c Germany
   d the author's great-grandparents

My favorite holiday is Thanksgiving. It is an American holiday and is on the fourth Thursday of November. On Thanksgiving, families eat a big dinner together. They have turkey, corn, potatoes, and pumpkin pie. Thanksgiving is a time to give thanks for the people and things in your life.

2 The topic of this paragraph is _____ .
   a holidays
   b turkey
   c Thanksgiving
   d people you are thankful for

Do you need a job? If you do, you will need a good resume. A resume is a document that lists your work experience. You write the details of your past jobs on a resume. These details include the dates you worked and the type of work you did. You send your resume to the company that has the job you want. Sending a resume is the first step in getting a job.

3 The topic of this paragraph is _____ .

    a jobs

    b resumes

    c companies

    d documents

Do you want to go to the top of the world? Mount Everest is 29,029 feet high and is the highest peak in the world. Mount Everest is a popular place to go for mountain climbers. It is a very difficult climb. The weather, the lack of oxygen, and the steep climb make Mount Everest one of the most difficult mountains in the world to climb.

4 The topic of this paragraph is _____ .

    a Mount Everest

    b mountain climbers

    c famous mountains

    d peaks

Practice 3

Read the topic choices and the paragraph. Then write the correct topic in the blank after the paragraph. There are two topics that will not be used.

celebrations	farmers' markets	greenways
exercise	birthday party	sushi

1 When we need something, we often go to the grocery store. However, a more interesting place to buy your food is at a farmers' market. Farmers' markets are all over the United States. Farmers bring their goods to the market to sell. Fruits and vegetables are not the only things for sale. Some farmers' markets have flowers, honey, and bread.

_____

2 My birthday was last week, and my friends gave me a surprise birthday party. I thought I was going to my friend's house for dinner, but when I got there, ten people jumped out from behind the couch! I was very surprised! We had cake, and my friends sang "Happy Birthday" to me. I will never forget that birthday party.

_____

3 Do you like to ride bikes and walk outside? Many cities around the United States are building greenways for people to enjoy. Greenways are natural walkways. No cars can go on a greenway, so it is very safe for people to walk or ride on them.

_____

4 One of my favorite foods is sushi. Many people think that sushi is just raw fish, but sushi is actually rice combined with vinegar and sugar. People like to put raw fish or vegetables on their sushi. Sushi is a nutritious and delicious meal!

_____

IDENTIFYING THE MAIN IDEA

Presentation

Identifying the Main Idea
The main idea is the most important point about a topic. To find the main idea, first find the topic and then ask, "What does the author want me to know about this topic?" The answer to that question is the main idea. The main idea can usually be found in the topic sentence.

Practice 1

Read the paragraph. Which statement describes the main idea? Circle the letter of the correct answer.

Do you notice the birds around you? Bird watching is a popular activity around the world. Some bird watchers observe birds with their eyes, but others use binoculars and telescopes. Often, birds can be heard but not seen. Many bird watchers know which bird it is just by its song.

1 a Bird watchers are interesting people.
  b Bird watching is difficult.
  c Birds are all around us.
  d Bird watching is a popular activity around the world.

It's a Saturday afternoon, and I can't see one child playing outside. Where are all the children? They are inside playing video games instead. Children today play too many video games. They are either playing a hand-held game, a computer game, or a game played on a television. These games hurt children's imaginations and diminish their childhoods.

2 a Children play too many video games.
  b Playing outside is fun.
  c Video games are popular.
  d Children don't play on Saturdays.

I thank my dog every day. My dog saved my life. When I was six years old, I fell down a big hole. My dog was with me. She went back to my house and barked at my parents. My parents did not know what she meant, but she continued to bark. After a while, my parents followed my dog and found me in the hole. I am very thankful for my dog.

3 **a** All dogs are heroes.
   b Holes can be dangerous.
   c The dog saved the author's life.
   d The author's dog barks a lot.

I love flea markets. A flea market is a kind of bazaar where people buy and sell low-priced merchandise, often used goods. Vendors sell items from tables or even from their cars. You can buy almost anything—household items, crafts, fresh produce, and specialty food items like homemade jams or pies. Flea markets are often annual or semiannual events but some are open every weekend. Almost every major city in the United States has a flea market. I go every year with my family. I like to buy unusual gifts there.

4 **a** It's nice to buy gifts for people.
   b A flea market is a bazaar where people buy and sell new, used, and homemade merchandise.
   c The crafts and food are very good at Christmas markets.
   d Almost every major city in the United States has a flea market.

I am a member of a book club. A book club is for people who like to read and talk about books. My book club meets once a month. Other book clubs meet more often. Some book clubs read only fiction, and some read only nonfiction. My book club reads both kinds of books.

5 **a** The author is a member of a book club.
   b A book club is for people who like to read and talk about books.
   c Some book clubs only read nonfiction books.
   d The author likes to read.

Practice 2

Read the essay. What is the main idea of each paragraph? Circle the letter of the correct answer.

(Paragraph 1) When you think of sharks, what do you see? Many people see a great white shark or a mako shark. The truth is that there are many kinds of sharks in the world. Some of them are very big, and some of them are very small. Some of them are aggressive, and some of them are very gentle. Great white sharks and mako sharks are very aggressive. Whale sharks and basking sharks are mostly harmless.

(Paragraph 2) Most sharks are carnivores and eat only meat. They live on a diet of fish and sea mammals. Dolphins and seals are their favorite food. Sharks also eat other sharks.

(Paragraph 3) Don't get near a shark's mouth! Sharks have very strong teeth. Their teeth are in long rows. Over time, their teeth get ground down or fall out. The teeth in the back row come forward to fill the empty spots. A shark may use over 20,000 teeth in its lifetime!

(Paragraph 4) Before dinosaurs walked Earth, sharks were swimming in the oceans. Sharks are very old. They have been on Earth for more than 450 million years. They are able to change and adapt to many situations. They are survivors.

(Paragraph 5) Are you afraid of sharks? Sharks are more afraid of you! There are many endangered sharks. Since 2004, 90 percent of the shark population has died. Sharks are one of the most endangered species on our planet.

(Paragraph 6) Sharks are endangered because people kill them. Commercial fishermen sell shark meat for food or other products. Their habitats are also endangered. People fish in all areas of the world. Sometimes, sharks get caught in fishing nets. The oceans are also dirty and polluted. This pollution is killing sharks and other sea life.

1 What is the main idea of paragraph 1?
  a Great white sharks are aggressive.
  b There are many kinds of sharks in the world.
  c Sharks are very big.
  d Whale sharks are very gentle.

2 What is the main idea of paragraph 2?
  a Most sharks are carnivores.
  b Sharks eat together.
  c Sharks eat fish and sea mammals.
  d Sharks like to eat dolphins and seals.

3 What is the main idea of paragraph 3?
  a Sharks' teeth grow in long rows.
  b Sharks' teeth fall out.
  c Sharks use over 20,000 teeth.
  d Sharks have strong teeth.

4 What is the main idea of paragraph 4?
  a Sharks are very old.
  b Sharks have been on Earth for 450 million years.
  c Sharks can swim.
  d Sharks were on Earth before dinosaurs.

5 What is the main idea of paragraph 5?

    a Many people are afraid of sharks.

    b Sharks are afraid of people.

    c The shark population is down 90 percent since 2004.

    d Many shark species are endangered.

6 What is the main idea of paragraph 6?

    a Many people kill sharks.

    b Commercial fishermen kill sharks.

    c People are the reason sharks are endangered.

    d Sharks get caught in fishing nets.

Practice 3

Read the essay. Underline the sentence in each paragraph that gives you the main idea.

1 When you think of sharks, what do you see? Many people see a great white shark or a mako shark. The truth is that there are many kinds of sharks in the world. Some of them are very big, and some of them are very small. Some of them are aggressive, and some of them are very gentle. Great white sharks and mako sharks are very aggressive. Whale sharks and basking sharks are mostly harmless.

2 Most sharks are carnivores and eat only meat. They live on a diet of fish and sea mammals. Dolphins and seals are their favorite food. Sharks also eat other sharks.

3 Don't get near a shark's mouth! Sharks have very strong teeth. Their teeth are in long rows. Over time, their teeth get ground down or fall out. The teeth in the back row come forward to fill the empty spots. A shark may use over 20,000 teeth in its lifetime!

4 Before dinosaurs walked Earth, sharks were swimming in the oceans. Sharks are very old. They have been on Earth for more than 450 million years. They are able to change and adapt to many situations. They are survivors.

5 Are you afraid of sharks? Sharks are more afraid of you! There are many endangered sharks. Since 2004, 90 percent of the shark population has died. Sharks are one of the most endangered species on our planet.

6 Sharks are endangered because people kill them. Commercial fishermen sell shark meat for food or other products. Their habitats are also endangered. People fish in all areas of the world. Sometimes, sharks get caught in fishing nets. The oceans are also dirty and polluted. This pollution is killing sharks and other sea life.

Scanning

SCANNING FOR LETTERS AND LETTER COMBINATIONS

Presentation

Scanning for Letters and Letter Combinations
It is important to recognize words quickly. Good readers see a word and know what it means right away. Practice looking at words quickly. Don't stop to think about each word. Train your mind to see a word and know what it is.

Practice 1

Read the list of words. Circle the letters of the words that begin with the key letters.

1 Which words begin with *l*?

a loud
b top
c lot
d toad
e load
f lick
g tick
h like

2 Which words begin with *d*?

a drink
b bed
c dead
d do
e dark
f bad
g bark
h different

3 Which words begin with *sh*?

a ship
b shop
c chop
d see
e shoe
f shark
g start
h sheep

4 Which words begin with *br*?

a book
b bread
c bird
d brain
e burn
f barn
g break
h broom

5 Which words begin with *th*?

a three
b tin
c through
d think
e tree
f they
g thin
h tray

6 Which words begin with *pr*?

a party
b pretty
c people
d present
e print
f person
g perfect
h professional

7 Which words begin with *wh*?

  a who

  b where

  c want

  d went

  e wish

  f when

  g what

  h wait

8 Which words begin with *fr*?

  a form

  b farm

  c friend

  d free

  e fire

  f from

  g fear

  h fry

Practice 2

Read the list of words. Circle the letters of the words that begin or end with the key letters.

1 Which words begin with *mi*?

  a me

  b mine

  c my

  d milk

  e middle

  f minute

  g more

  h mice

2 Which words begin with *ta*?

  a tall

  b there

  c take

  d talk

  e true

  f table

  g train

  h taste

3 Which words begin with *ha*?

  a head

  b hair

  c hit

  d hotel

  e hammer

  f hard

  g hot

  h have

4 Which words begin with *le*?

  a lead

  b learn

  c last

  d lot

  e left

  f letter

  g likely

  h lace

5 Which words end with *er*?

  a teacher

  b actor

  c more

  d there

  e either

  f better

  g summer

  h their

6 Which words end with *ck*?

  a sick

  b pitch

  c bike

  d clock

  e chicken

  f back

  g like

  h sock

7 Which words end with *th*?

a tooth
b bottle
c mother
d math
e left
f feather
g mouth
h bath

8 Which words end with *ing*?

a swimming
b during
c strong
d sing
e wrong
f nothing
g bang
h bring

SCANNING FOR KEY WORDS AND PHRASES

Presentation

Scanning for Key Words

Scanning is a way to read quickly to find key words and information. To scan, move your eyes quickly across the page until you find the key words or information. Before you scan, think about the information you are looking for. If you are looking for a date, scan for numbers on the page.

Practice 1

Read the list of words. Circle the letters of the words that are the same.

1
a from
b fair
c from
d form
e front
f from
g fresh
h from

2
a out
b owl
c hour
d our
e only
f our
g or
h our

3
a knee
b know
c known
d know
e now
f knock
g know
h new

4
a and
b any
c also
d and
e also
f after
g and
h an

5
a have
b has
c her
d has
e his
f has
g hasn't
h had

6
a did
b do
c didn't
d does
e did
f day
g don't
h did

7
 a those
 b there
 c that
 d that
 e then
 f that
 g they
 h these

8
 a its
 b it
 c it's
 d is
 e its
 f if
 g in
 h its

Presentation

Scanning for Key Phrases

Scanning is a way to read quickly to find key words and information. To scan, move your eyes quickly across the page until you find the key words or information. Before you scan, think about the information you are looking for. If you are looking for a date, scan for numbers on the page. Sometimes, words are used together in a sentence as a phrase. Good readers learn to read words together as phrases.

Practice 2

Look at the phrases in the box. Write the phrases in the blanks to match the items in the list below. You will not use all of the phrases.

pick out	turn on	pick up	in night
get out	clean out	turn in	get up
turn off	save time	at night	safe time
get in	cross off	pick on	across from
done over	do over	at light	same time
clean up	cross from	do again	

1 Get out _____

2 Turn on _____

3 Clean up _____

4 Pick up _____

5 Save time _____

6 At night _____

7 Across from _____

8 Do over _____

Presentation

Scanning for Key Words and Phrases in a Paragraph

Scanning is a way to read quickly to find key words and information. To scan a paragraph for specific information, follow these steps:

• Think about the information you are looking for. If you are looking for a date, scan for numbers. If you are looking for a person, scan for names.

• Only pay attention to the word or phrase you are looking for. Don't read the text for meaning.

• Move your eyes quickly across the page until you find the information.

Practice 3

Scan the paragraph. Underline the key word or phrase.

1 Underline the key word *has*.

My favorite sport is lacrosse. Lacrosse is a team sport and was originally a Native American game. It is played with a stick and a ball. The stick has a net on it and is designed to catch and hold the lacrosse ball. Lacrosse is very popular in Canada and the United States.

2 Underline the key word *just*.

Do you notice the birds around you? Bird watching is a popular activity around the world. Some bird watchers observe birds with their eyes, but others use binoculars and telescopes. Often, birds can be heard but not seen. Many bird watchers know which bird it is just by its song.

3 Underline the key word *bring*.

When we need something, we often go to the grocery store. However, a more interesting place to buy your food is at a farmers' market. Farmers' markets are all over the United States. Farmers bring their goods to the market to sell. Fruits and vegetables are not the only things for sale. Some farmers' markets have flowers, honey, and bread.

4 Underline the key phrase *every night*.

My family goes on a summer vacation every year. Last summer, we went camping at a nearby lake. We brought our boat with us, so every day we relaxed and swam in the lake. Every night, we had a big campfire. We roasted hot dogs and marshmallows over the fire and sang songs. We had a great time.

5 Underline the key phrase *once a month*.

I am a member of a book club. A book club is for people who like to read and talk about books. My book club meets once a month. Other book clubs meet more often. Some book clubs read only fiction, and some read only nonfiction. My book club reads both kinds of books.

Practice 4

Scan the paragraph. Underline the key words.

1 Underline the key word *in*.

I love flea markets. A flea market is a group of shops and booths. You can find almost anything from secondhand goods to crafts to food in a flea market. They are often only open on weekends. Flea markets began in rural areas, but now many cities in the United States have them, too. I go every year with my family. I like to look for unusual gifts there.

2 Underline the key word *is*.

One of my favorite foods is sushi. Many people think that sushi is raw fish, but sushi is actually rice combined with vinegar and sugar. People like to put raw fish or vegetables on their sushi, though. Sushi is a nutritious and delicious meal!

3 Underline the key word *you*.

Do you need a job? If you do, you will need a good resume. A resume is a document that lists your work experience. You write the details of your past jobs on a resume. The details include the dates you worked and the type of work you did. You send your resume to the company that has the job you want. Sending a resume is the first step in getting a job.

4 Underline the key word *they*.

My great-grandparents were born in Germany. After they got married, they came to the United States in 1882. They wanted a better life. My great-grandfather worked as a baker, and my great-grandmother made dresses. They worked very hard and saved their money. They liked their new life in the United States.

5 Underline the key word *study*.

It's important to have good study habits at home. There are many distractions at home, and it can be hard to study. Study in an area without a television or radio. Television and radio can be very distracting. Also, turn off your phone when you study. A phone call can take you away from your studies.

SCANNING FOR INFORMATION

Presentation

Scanning for Information

Scanning is a way to read quickly to find key words and information. To scan a paragraph for specific information, follow these steps:

- Think about the information you are looking for. If you are looking for a date, scan for numbers. If you are looking for a person, scan for names.
- Only pay attention to the word or phrase you are looking for. Don't read the text for meaning.
- Move your eyes quickly across the page until you find the information.

Practice 1

Look at the bus schedule. Read the question. Circle the letter of the correct answer.

1 What school does the bus serve?
- **a** Preston University
- **b** East Campus
- **c** Alexander Building
- **d** Anderson Building
- **e** West Campus

Preston University
East Campus to West Campus
Buses run from 7:00 A.M.–5:00 P.M.,
Monday through Friday

East Campus	Alexander Building	Anderson Building	West Campus
7:00	7:03	7:07	7:15
7:10	7:13	7:17	7:25
7:20	7:23	7:27	7:35
7:30	7:33	7:37	7:45
7:40	7:43	7:47	7:55
7:50	7:53	7:57	8:05
8:00	8:03	8:07	8:15

2 What time does the bus start in the morning from East Campus?
- **a** Buses run from 7:00 A.M.– 5:00 P.M.
- **b** Monday through Friday
- **c** 7:00
- **d** 7:03
- **e** 7:07
- **f** 7:15
- **g** 7:10

3 Where is the second stop on the route?
- **a** Preston University
- **b** East Campus
- **c** Alexander Building
- **d** Anderson Building
- **e** West Campus

4 Which days does the bus run?
- **a** East Campus to West Campus
- **b** Buses run from 7:00 A.M.–5:00 P.M.
- **c** Monday through Friday
- **d** East Campus
- **e** West Campus

5 What is the last stop on the route?
- **a** Preston University
- **b** East Campus to West Campus
- **c** East Campus
- **d** Alexander Building
- **e** Anderson Building
- **f** West Campus

Practice 2

Look at the brochure. Read the question. Circle the letter of the correct answer.

Town of Cary
Number of Players in Sports Programs

Sport	Number of Players, 2008	Number of Players, 2013
Soccer	820	1650
Football	980	760
Baseball	1025	940
Lacrosse	210	200
Basketball	960	930

1 What is the chart about?
   a Town of Cary
   b number of players in sports programs
   c sports
   d football
   e baseball
   f basketball

2 How many sports programs does the town of Cary have?
   a 5
   b 820
   c 980
   d 1,025
   e 200
   f 960

3 Which sport had the most players in 2008?
   a soccer
   b football
   c baseball
   d lacrosse
   e basketball

4 How many people played football in 2013?
   a 1,650
   b 980
   c 760
   d 940
   e 200
   f 930

5 Which sport became more popular between 2008 and 2013?
   a football
   b soccer
   c baseball
   d lacrosse
   e basketball

Practice 3

Look at the schedule. Read the question. Circle the letter of the correct answer.

Home and Garden Conference
Class Schedule
May 12–13
Saturday Schedule

Morning Classes	Class Description	Time	Room
Fence It In!	Do you have kids or a dog? Do you need to fence in your yard? It's easy! Come and learn how to do it yourself.	9:00	202
Gorgeous Grass	Learn what kind of grass you need for your yard.	9:00	204
New for Dinner	Are you tired of the same food for dinner? Come and learn some new ideas!	9:00	206
Bonsai!	Japanese bonsai trees make any garden beautiful. Come and learn how to grow a bonsai tree.	10:00	202
Easy Snacks	Do you have children? Are they always hungry? Learn how to make easy, nutritious snacks.	10:00	204
A New Color	Are you tired of the same color on your walls? Paint your walls! It's easy to get a new look and feel for your home.	10:00	206
Organize It!	Is it difficult to find anything? You need help to clean up your house. Come and learn some new tricks for home organization.	11:00	202
Perfect Pasta	Everybody loves spaghetti! Come and learn some new spaghetti recipes. Your family will be happy!	11:00	204
Move It!	New furniture is expensive. You don't need to buy anything new. Just move the furniture you have! Move your couch here and your table there, and get a new look for your home.	11:00	206
12:00: Lunch is served in Conference Room 200			
Afternoon Classes	Class Description	Time	Room
Flower Arrangements			

1 What is the name of the conference?

  a Fence It In!
  b Home and Garden
  c Gorgeous Grass
  d 10:00

2 What time is the class on making spaghetti?

  a 10:00
  b 9:00
  c 11:00
  d 204

3 What room number is the class on paint?

  a 206
  b A New Color
  c 10:00
  d 204

4 Which class is about snacks?

  a Perfect Pasta
  b Organize It!
  c Easy Snacks
  d New for Dinner

5 Which class is about Japanese trees?

  a A New Color
  b Bonsai!
  c Move It!
  d Fence It In!

Practice 4

Read each question. Scan the text for the answer. Do not read the whole text. Then circle the letter of the correct answer.

(Paragraph 1) When you think of sharks, what do you see? Many people see a great white shark or a mako shark. The truth is that there are many kinds of sharks in the world. Some of them are very big, and some of them are very small. Some of them are aggressive, and some of them are very gentle. Great white sharks and mako sharks are very aggressive. Whale sharks and basking sharks are mostly harmless.

(Paragraph 2) Most sharks are carnivores and eat only meat. They live on a diet of fish and sea mammals. Dolphins and seals are their favorite food. Sharks even eat other sharks.

(Paragraph 3) Don't get near a shark's mouth! Sharks have very strong teeth. Their teeth are in long rows. Over time, their teeth get ground down or fall out. The teeth in the back row come forward to fill the empty spots. A shark may use over 20,000 teeth in its lifetime!

(Paragraph 4) Before dinosaurs walked Earth, sharks were swimming in the oceans. Sharks are very old. They have been on Earth for more than 450 million years. They are able to change and adapt to many situations. They are survivors.

(Paragraph 5) Are you afraid of sharks? Sharks are more afraid of you! There are many endangered sharks. Since 2004, 90 percent of the shark population has died. Sharks are one of the most endangered species on our planet.

(Paragraph 6) Sharks are endangered because people kill them. Commercial fishermen sell shark meat for food or other products. Their habitats are also endangered. People fish in all areas of the world. Sometimes, sharks get caught in fishing nets. The oceans are also dirty and polluted. This pollution is killing sharks and other sea life.

1 Dolphins and seals are sharks' favorite food.

   a true   **b** false

2 Sharks don't use very many teeth during their lifetimes.

   a true   **b** false

3 Sharks are young. They have only been on Earth for 20,000 years.

   a true   **b** false

4 Whale sharks are less aggressive than great white sharks.

   a true   **b** false

5 Many shark species are endangered.

   a true   **b** false

Recognizing Patterns
RECOGNIZING TIME ORDER

Presentation

Recognizing Time Order

Many texts have some kind of order. Time order is the most common type of order in texts. The writer tells you what happened first, second, third, and so on. Look for clues that give information about the order of events. Dates, times, and key words help you understand the order. Some common time order words are *first, second, third, then, next, after, later, before, finally,* and *at last.*

Practice 1

Read the paragraph. Determine the order of each event. Then write the sentences in the correct order.

Before you do a presentation in front of your class, there are some things you need to do. First, you need to think of a topic idea. Ask yourself, "What do you want to talk about?" Next, research your topic. Go online and take notes on your topic. Then write your presentation. You may need to write several drafts of your presentation before it's complete. After it is complete, practice your presentation. Practice in front of your family. Finally, you are ready to give your presentation.

1

Research your topic.	Give your presentation.	Practice your presentation.
Think of a topic idea.	Write your presentation.	

a _____

b _____

c _____

d _____

e _____

Last summer was terrible for Tom. First, he got sick. He was sick for two weeks. After he got better, he broke his finger playing basketball. Then he went camping with his family. While camping, he burned his foot on the fire. Finally, at the end of the summer, he fell off his bicycle and broke his arm. Tom was happy when school started!

2

| Tom broke his finger. | School started. | Tom broke his arm. |
| | Tom got sick. | Tom burned his foot. |

a _____

b _____

c _____

d _____

e _____

There once was a strong lion in the jungle. The other animals were afraid of the lion. One day, the lion caught a mouse. Before the lion opened his mouth to eat him, the mouse said, "Let me go and someday I will help you." The lion thought this was very funny. How could a little mouse help a strong lion? Then the lion decided to let the mouse go. A month later, some hunters caught the lion in a net. Before the hunters came back, the mouse saw the lion in the net. He chewed through the net, and the lion was free. Then the lion thanked the mouse. He realized that a small animal can be helpful, too. In the end, they became good friends.

3

| The mouse said, "Let me go." | The mouse chewed through the net. | The lion and mouse became friends. |
| The lion let the mouse go. | Hunters caught the lion in a net. | |

a _____

b _____

c _____

d _____

e _____

Practice 2

Part 1

Read the paragraph. Determine the sequence of each event. Then draw lines to match the sentences to the correct sequence.

The party at Nancy's house is next week. To get there, first turn right on Main Street. Then go two miles and turn left on Market Street. After the first traffic light, turn left on River Road. Then go straight for four miles. After four miles, look for a park on your left. After the park, turn left on Park Drive. Then go up the hill. Nancy's house is on the right. Park your car in her driveway.

First	Turn left on River Road.
Second	Park your car in her driveway.
Third	Go two miles and turn left on Market Street.
Fourth	Go straight for four miles.
Fifth	Look for a park on your left.
Sixth	Turn left on Park Drive.
Seventh	Turn right on Main Street.

Part 2

Read the paragraph. Determine the sequence of each event. Then draw lines to match the sentences to the correct sequence.

I clean my apartment every Saturday morning. First, I pick up all of the papers on my desk and table. There are a lot of papers from school and work. After I pick up my papers, I throw the garbage out. Next, I vacuum the floors. I have a dog, and there is a lot of dog hair on the floor. After I vacuum, I clean the kitchen. I wash the dishes first, and then I wash the stove and sink. Finally, I wash and dry my clothes. Finally, after my clothes are dry, I relax! I can begin my weekend!

First	Wash the dishes.
Second	Throw the garbage out.
Third	Pick up all of the papers.
Fourth	Clean the kitchen.
Fifth	Relax and begin the weekend.
Sixth	Vacuum the floors.
Seventh	Wash the stove and sink.
Eighth	Wash and dry clothes.

Part 3

Read the paragraph. Determine the sequence of each event. Then draw lines to match the sentences to the correct sequence.

Candles are nice, but they can drip wax on your clothes. Follow these steps to get candle wax off of your shirt. First, get an iron and an ironing board. Second, turn the iron on. Wait until it is hot. Then put your shirt on the ironing board. Next, get a paper bag. Cover the wax spot on your shirt with the paper bag. Then move the iron over the paper bag. The wax melts onto the paper bag. Continue until all the wax is gone.

First	Continue until all the wax is gone.
Second	Move the iron over the paper bag.
Third	Get an iron and an ironing board.
Fourth	Wait until the iron is hot.
Fifth	Turn the iron on.
Sixth	Cover the wax spot with the paper bag.
Seventh	Put your shirt on the ironing board.

Practice 3

Read the paragraph. Determine the order of each event. Then write the sentences in the correct order.

Michelle has many life experiences. After Michelle finished college, she moved to Tokyo. She worked as an English teacher. At first, she didn't like Tokyo. It was too big, and there were so many people. After a few months, she learned more Japanese and met some Japanese people. They were all very kind to her. After she made Japanese friends, she learned a lot about the culture, and she really enjoyed living in Tokyo. After two years of working there, she finally went home. She always remembers her wonderful experiences in Japan.

1

Michelle moved to Tokyo.	Michelle finished college.	She learned more Japanese and made Japanese friends.	Michelle left Tokyo to go home.
She learned about the culture and enjoyed living in Tokyo.	She didn't like Tokyo.		

a _____

b _____

c _____

d _____

e _____

f _____

I often go to the movie theater on Academy Street. It wasn't always a movie theater. At first, it was a concert hall. Many musicians played there a long time ago. Then the war started, and there wasn't any money for concerts. The building was empty for many years. After the war, the owners made it into a shoe store. Then they got old and sold it. Next, it became a restaurant. It was a restaurant for thirty years. After the restaurant owners died, the town bought the building. They made it into a movie theater. Now, many people go there to see movies.

2

The town bought the building. The war started. The building was a concert hall.	The building became a movie theater. People go there to watch movies.	The building was a restaurant for thirty years. The building became a shoe store.

a _____

b _____

c _____

d _____

e _____

f _____

g _____

When I was young, we moved around a lot. I lived in many different countries. I was born in the United States. When I was two, we moved to Spain. I lived in Spain until I was five years old. Then we moved to India. We lived in New Delhi for four years. After that, we lived in Mexico for five years. Next, we moved to Canada. We lived there until last year. Now I live in California. I am going to a university in San Francisco. I don't think I want to move ever again!

3

I was born in the United States. I lived in Mexico for five years.	I lived in Canada. I lived in India for four years. I live in California.	I lived in Spain until I was five years old. My family moved to Spain.

a _____

b _____

c _____

d _____

e _____

f _____

g _____

LISTING PATTERN

Presentation

Listing Pattern

Many texts give examples, details, and facts that support the main idea. All of the facts are important, so the order of the list doesn't matter. In other words, changing the order of the details does not change the meaning of the paragraph.

A writer uses key words to list or introduce the details. Here are some common words used for listing: *one, for example, and, also, another, in addition, other.*

Practice 1

Read the paragraph. How many examples related to the main idea are there? Circle the letter of the correct number of examples in the paragraph.

I love my grandmother. She has so many wonderful qualities. For example, she is very kind. She helps everyone, and she never asks for anything in return. Also, she is very smart. She went to Harvard University and was a professor for thirty years. In addition to being smart, my grandmother is very humble. She doesn't tell people about all the things she has done. There are so many good things about my grandmother. I want to be just like her.

1 a 2
b 3
c 4
d 5

Every weekend, my friends and I go out for dinner. We have many good restaurants in our city. For example, there is a great Chinese restaurant downtown. I really like the dumplings there. In addition to the Chinese restaurant, there is a little noodle shop near my house. The noodles there are really good, the food is always inexpensive, and it arrives at the table fast. Also, there is a nice French restaurant. It's a little expensive, but it is fun to go there for special occasions. Another favorite restaurant is the Brazilian steak house. They have many kinds of meat on their menu. We are going there this weekend. I can't wait!

2 a 2
  b 3
  c 4
  d 5

My brother's new car has a lot of nice features. For example, it has a sun roof. He can open up the top of the car and see the sky. Another good feature is the leather seats. Leather is so comfortable. Also, the seats have a heater! In the winter, the seats are warm. Other good parts about his car are the color, the speed, and the radio. I like it a lot. I want one, too!

3 a 3
  b 4
  c 5
  d 6

I am in my last year at the university. My class schedule this year is really full. One of my most difficult classes is math. I don't like math very much, and I'm having a hard time in this class. Another difficult class is World History. The teacher gives many tests in that class. Not all of my classes are hard. I have several easy ones. English, Social Studies, and Geography are all easy and fun.

4 a 3
  b 4
  c 5
  d 6

There are so many things to do and see in New York City. One great thing to do is to go to the Statue of Liberty. Another great place to visit is Central Park. I love to walk through there. Also, the Broadway shows are fun to watch. I saw a musical, and it was fantastic. Other good things about the city are the restaurants. You can get any kind of food you want. In addition to the restaurants, the street vendors are also a great part of New York.

5 a 3
  b 4
  c 5
  d 6

Practice 2

Read the paragraph. Underline the sentences that list examples.

1 I love my grandmother. She has so many wonderful qualities. For example, she is very kind. She helps everyone, and she never asks for anything in return. Also, she is very smart. She went to Harvard University and was a professor for thirty years. In addition to being smart, my grandmother is very humble. She doesn't tell people about all the things she has done. There are so many good things about my grandmother. I want to be just like her.

2 Every weekend, my friends and I go out for dinner. We have many good restaurants in our city. For example, there is a great Chinese restaurant downtown. I really like the dumplings there. In addition to the Chinese restaurant, there is a little noodle shop near my house. The noodles there are really good, the food is always inexpensive, and it arrives at the table fast. Also, there is a nice French restaurant. It's a little expensive, but it is fun to go there for special occasions. Another favorite restaurant is the Brazilian steak house. They have many kinds of meat on their menu. We are going there this weekend. I can't wait!

3 My brother's new car has a lot of nice features. For example, it has a sun roof. He can open up the top of the car and see the sky. Another good feature is the leather seats. Leather is so comfortable. Also, the seats have a heater! In the winter, the seats are warm. Other good parts about his car are the color, the speed, and the radio. I like it a lot. I want one, too!

4 I am in my last year at the university. My class schedule this year is really full. One of my most difficult classes is math. I don't like math very much, and I'm having a hard time in this class. Another difficult class is World History. The teacher gives many tests in that class. Not all of my classes are hard. I have several easy ones. English, Social Studies, and Geography are all easy and fun.

5 There are so many things to do and see in New York City. One great thing to do is to go to the Statue of Liberty. Another great place to visit is Central Park. I love to walk through there. Also, the Broadway shows are fun to watch. I saw a musical, and it was fantastic. Other good things about the city are the restaurants. You can get any kind of food you want. In addition to the restaurants, the street vendors are also a great part of New York.

Practice 3

Read the paragraph. Underline the sentences that list examples.

1 There are many benefits to riding the bus to work. For example, taking the bus is inexpensive. It costs less than a dollar to get from one side of town to another. Also, you can get things done on a bus. You can read, work, or even sleep! Another reason to take the bus is the convenience. When you get to your bus stop, you don't have to find a parking spot. Parking spots are hard to find in a city. In addition, riding the bus can be fun. You can meet many nice people on the bus. I take the bus every day, and I like it.

2 When I lived in Spain, I noticed several things that were different from my life in the United States. One example is the schedule. In Spain, people eat their dinner at 10:00 at night. Also, they go to bed very late at night. Another example is the women's clothing. They wear beautiful clothes every day. They also wear beautiful shoes everywhere they go. Another difference is how people greet one another. People kiss each other once on both cheeks. This was very different for me.

SEQUENCE PATTERN

Presentation

Sequence Pattern

Many texts have some kind of order. A common way to order a text is through sequence. A writer tells what happened first, second, and so forth.

A writer uses key words to make the sequence explicit. Here are some common words used for sequencing: *after, as soon as, before, one day, then, the next day, when, last night, last month, yesterday, at last.*

Practice 1

Read the paragraph. Underline the sentences that have a sequence key word.

1 One day, I found a black cat in my yard. It looked hungry, so I took it inside and gave it some milk and food. After the cat ate, it jumped in my lap and fell asleep. As soon as it woke up, it purred and drank some more milk. It was such a cute cat. I wanted to keep it. My mom said that we needed to find its home. The next day, we saw a sign for a missing cat. We called the number, and the people came to see the cat. As soon as the people saw the cat, they knew it was their lost cat. After they took the cat home, I was very sad. I had the cat for only a day, but I really loved her.

2 Last week was my birthday. My friends gave me a surprise birthday party. I went to my friend's house for dinner. As soon as I got there, all of my friends jumped out from behind the couch. I was so surprised! Before they gave me my presents, they sang "Happy Birthday" to me. I got some really cool presents. After we ate, we played some music and had a dance party. It was so much fun! The next day, I was tired but very happy! My friends are the best!

3 Once, there was a mouse family that lived in a stone wall. When it was time for the daughter mouse to get married, the father mouse went out to look for a husband. He wanted the best husband for his daughter. He went to the sun, but the sun said that the cloud was better. The cloud can cover the sun. Then the mouse asked the cloud, but the cloud said that the wind was better. The wind can blow the cloud. Next, he went to the wind. The wind said that the wall is better. The wind can't move the wall. At last, he went to the wall. The wall said that the mouse was better. The mouse can dig holes in the wall. The next day, the daughter married a handsome mouse. They lived happily ever after.

Practice 2

Read the paragraph. Determine the order of each event. Then write the sentences in the correct order.

One day, I found a black cat in my yard. It looked hungry, so I took it inside and gave it some milk and food. After the cat ate, it jumped in my lap and fell asleep. As soon as it woke up, it purred and drank some milk. It was such a cute cat. I wanted to keep it. My mom said that we needed to find its home. The next day, we saw a sign for a missing cat. We called the number, and the people came to see the cat. As soon as the people saw the cat, they knew it was their lost cat. After they took the cat home, I was very sad. I had the cat for only a day, but I really loved her.

1

| The cat ate.
The people saw the cat.
I saw a sign for a missing cat. | I found a black cat in my yard.
They knew it was their cat. | The cat woke up and drank some milk.
They took the cat home. | The cat jumped in my lap and fell asleep. |

a _____

b _____

c _____

d _____

e _____

f _____

g _____

h _____

Last week was my birthday. My friends gave me a surprise birthday party. I went to my friend's house for dinner. As soon as I got there, all of my friends jumped out from behind the couch. I was so surprised! Before they gave me my presents, they sang "Happy Birthday" to me. I got some really cool presents. After we ate, we played some music and had a dance party. It was so much fun! The next day, I was tired but very happy! My friends are the best!

2

| It was my birthday.
We had a dance party.
My friends sang "Happy Birthday." | We ate.
I went to my friend's house for dinner.
I was tired but happy. | My friends gave me presents.
All of my friends jumped out. |

a _____

b _____

c _____

d _____

e _____

f _____

g _____

h _____

Once there was a mouse family that lived in a stone wall. When it was time for the daughter mouse to get married, the father mouse went out to look for a husband. He wanted the best husband for his daughter. He went to the sun, but the sun said that the cloud was better. The cloud can cover the sun. Then the mouse asked the cloud, but the cloud said that the wind was better. The wind can blow the cloud. Next, he went to the wind. The wind said that the wall is better. The wind can't move the wall. At last, he went to the wall. The wall said that the mouse was better. The mouse can dig holes in the wall. The next day, the daughter married a handsome mouse. They lived happily ever after.

3

The father mouse went to look for a husband.	The father went to the sun.	It was time for the daughter to marry.	The father went to the cloud.
The father went to the wind.	The father went to the wall.	The daughter married a handsome mouse.	

a _____

b _____

c _____

d _____

e _____

f _____

g _____

Practice 3

Part 1

Read the story. Identify the sequence. Then draw lines to match the sentences to the correct sequence.

One day, a shop owner saw a man steal some food from his store. Before the man left the store, the owner caught him. The owner asked him why he had stolen the food. The man said that he needed it to feed his family. He said he had lost his job and had no money. As soon as the owner heard the story, he let him go with the food. Before the man left, however, the owner told him to come back the next day. The man returned, and the owner gave him a job. After he got the job, the man never stole again.

First	The man left the store.
Second	The owner let the man go and told him to come back tomorrow.
Third	The owner gave the man a job.
Fourth	The man came back.
Fifth	The owner listened to the man's story.
Sixth	A shop owner saw a man steal from his store.
Seventh	The owner caught the man.

Part 2

Read the paragraph. Identify the sequence. Then draw lines to match the sentences to the correct sequence.

Once, there was a grasshopper who didn't like to work. He spent his time singing and playing music all day long. One day, he saw an ant. The ant was very busy. He was carrying food on his back. When the grasshopper saw the ant, he said, "Let's have some fun!" The ant told the grasshopper that he had to prepare for the winter. Then the grasshopper said, "Winter is many months away." The next day, the grasshopper saw the ant again. He was working hard again. The grasshopper said, "All you do is work all day. You're boring!" The ant continued his work. He worked hard all summer and fall. The grasshopper continued his play. He played all summer and fall. As soon as winter came, the ant was happy in his warm house with his food. When the grasshopper asked the ant for some food, the ant said, "Next time, you need to prepare!"

First	The grasshopper asked for food.
Second	The grasshopper said, "Let's have some fun."
Third	The ant was happy in his warm house.
Fourth	The grasshopper said, "Winter is many months away."
Fifth	Winter came.
Sixth	The ant said, "Next time, you need to prepare."
Seventh	The grasshopper saw an ant.

Part 3

Read the paragraph. Identify the sequence. Then draw lines to match the sentences to the correct sequence.

Last month, Tom bought a motorcycle. He rode it all over town. He wanted to go very fast. One day, he took it to a country road and drove very fast. As he went around a corner, a police officer's car was behind a tree. When the police officer saw Tom speeding, he turned on his lights and pulled him over to the side of the road. The next day, Tom went to the judge. The judge asked him, "Do you have anything to say?" Tom said, "I am innocent." The judge asked, "Didn't you see the speed limit sign? You were going 80 mph in a 50 mph zone." Tom replied, "Sir, how could I read the sign when I was driving so fast?" The judge laughed, but after that, he gave Tom a speeding ticket.

First	A police officer saw Tom.
Second	The judge gave Tom a speeding ticket.
Third	Tom bought a motorcycle.
Fourth	Tom went to the judge.
Fifth	The judge laughed.
Sixth	Tom drove very fast.
Seventh	Tom took his motorcycle to a country road.
Eighth	A police officer pulled Tom over to the side of the road.

Making Inferences

MAKING INFERENCES FROM PICTURES

Presentation

Making Inferences from Pictures

An inference is like a guess. When you see a picture, you can guess—or make an inference—about the things in the picture. You also make inferences based on your personal experiences. You can use what you see and know about a situation to make an inference. Inferences give you clues into what you are going to read.

Practice 1

Make an inference about the picture. Circle the letter of the correct answer.

1 This girl is _____ .

   a proud

   b afraid

   c sad

   d bored

   e sleepy

   f happy

   g hungry

2 The parents are _____ .

   a sad

   b afraid

   c angry

   d proud

   e bored

   f sleepy

   g hungry

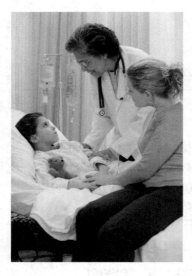

3 This girl is _____ .

   a afraid
   b angry
   c proud
   d bored
   e sleepy
   f happy
   g hungry

4 These children are _____ .

   a sad
   b proud
   c afraid
   d angry
   e bored
   f happy
   g hungry

5 This man is _____ .

   a proud
   b afraid
   c angry
   d bored
   e lively
   f happy
   g hungry

6 This man is _____ .

   a sad
   b proud
   c afraid
   d angry
   e sleepy
   f happy
   g hungry

Practice 2

Look at the picture. Read the question. Circle the letter of the correct answer.

1 Where are these people?

    a They are on a street near their house.

    b They are at the girl's school.

    c They are on a street in a big city.

    d They are in front of a store.

2 What are these people doing?

    a They are taking a walk.

    b They are looking for their dog.

    c They are hiking in the mountains.

    d They are looking at flowers.

3 What are these people saying?

    a They are saying hello to a neighbor.

    b They are singing a song.

    c They are telling a story.

    d They are calling out their dog's name.

4 How do these people feel?

    a They are worried.

    b They are happy.

    c They are hungry.

    d They are proud.

Practice 3

Look at the picture. Read the question. Circle the letter of the correct answer.

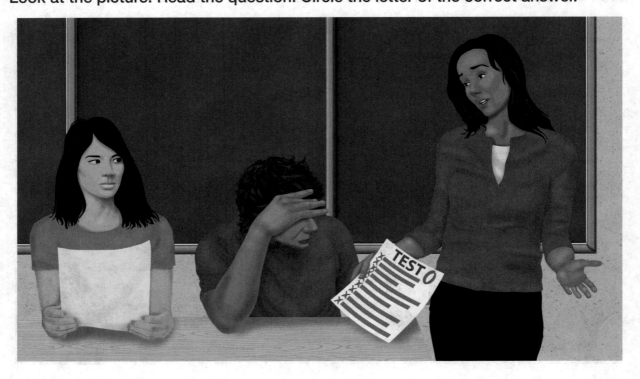

1 Where is this man?
  a He is at his house.
  b He is at a restaurant.
  c He is in a library.
  d He is in a classroom.

2 What is this man doing?
  a He is taking a test.
  b He is getting his test back from the teacher.
  c He is listening to his teacher.
  d He is talking to his teacher.

3 How does the man feel?
  a He feels proud.
  b He feels lonely.
  c He feels embarrassed.
  d He feels sleepy.

4 How does the woman feel?
  a She is proud of the man.
  b She is disappointed in the man.
  c She is angry at the man.
  d She is happy for the man.

MAKING INFERENCES FROM RIDDLES

> **Presentation**
>
> **Making Inferences from Riddles**
>
> An inference is similar to a guess. We make inferences based on our personal experiences, the available information, and our own knowledge about a given topic.
>
> Many times, a writer doesn't give all of the information about a situation. Good readers make inferences about the missing information. Inferences can help us understand a text better and read it faster.

Practice 1

Read the riddle. Then make an inference about the answer.

1 It lives on the ground and in trees. It is very long. Some people are afraid of it. It has no legs.

What is it?
  a bug
  b snake
  c fish
  d lizard

2 You put this in a salad. Some people put it on sandwiches. It's leafy and green. It's nutritious.

What is it?
  a tomato
  b lemon
  c cucumber
  d lettuce

3 This person talks to people and asks questions. This person listens to people's stories. This person writes stories. This person's stories can go in the newspaper.

What is this person's job?
  a reporter
  b photographer
  c office manager
  d custodian

4 It's red. Some people put it on their hot dogs. It's made from tomatoes. It's not a solid.

What is it?
  a cheese
  b salt
  c ketchup
  d mustard

5 It's small and shy. It eats bugs. It has eight legs. It lives in a web.

What is it?
  a bird
  b octopus
  c butterfly
  d spider

6 This person works with water. This person climbs ladders. This person saves people. This person drives a big truck.

What is this person's job?
  a diver
  b police officer
  c firefighter
  d gardener

Practice 2

Read the riddle. Make an inference. Write the words in the blank after the correct riddle. You will not use all the words.

book	pencil	notebook
table	eraser	chair
computer	paper	whiteboard

1 You use this to write. You can erase with it. Students often use this. _____

2 You write on this. It's big. It hangs on a wall. _____

3 You write on this. It's made from trees. It's in books. _____

4 It has four legs. It has a seat. You sit on it. _____

5 You use this for writing. You put your legs under it. You sit at it. _____

6 It helps you remove mistakes. It takes away something you've written. You hold it in your hand. _____

7 You learn from it. It has many words. Somebody wrote it. _____

8 It helps you send messages. You can search on it. You type on it. _____

park	bus stop	bank
school	library	grocery store
airport	mall	restaurant

9 You shouldn't be loud here. You can borrow books from here. You can do research here. _____

10 There are aisles. You push a cart here. There are many kinds of food here. _____

11 It is outside. There are many trees. People come here to relax. _____

12 People bring you food here. You choose what you want. You eat here. _____

13 You learn here. You don't go here on holidays. You get grades here. _____

14 It is safe to keep your things here. You can put things in and take things out. It has a lot of money. _____

15 You wait here. You get on a big vehicle here. It is outside. _____

16 It has many shops inside. It has big hallways. You can buy clothes, shoes, and toys here. _____

MAKING INFERENCES FROM CONVERSATIONS AND STORIES

Presentation

Making Inferences from Conversations

An inference is similar to a guess. We make inferences based on our personal experiences, available information, and our own knowledge about a given topic.

Many times, a writer doesn't give all of the information about a situation. Good readers make inferences about the missing information. Inferences can help us understand a text better and read it faster.

Practice 1

Read the conversation and question. Then circle the letter of the correct answer.

Conversation 1

A: Please hand in your reports.

B: Excuse me, I don't have mine.

A: Where is it?

B: At home.

A: It was due today. I'm going to have to give you a lower grade.

B: I understand. I'll bring it tomorrow. Please excuse me.

A: OK. Next time, pay attention to due dates!

1 Where are these people?
  a They're at work.
  b They're at home.
  c They're at school.
  d They're at a store.

2 Who are these people?
  a A is a boss. **B** is a worker.
  b A is a teacher. **B** is a student.
  c A is a student. **B** is a teacher.
  d A is a mother. **B** is a son.

3 What are these people talking about?
  a B forgot his report.
  b B did poorly on a test.
  c A is giving back a report.
  d A is teaching about reports.

4 How does **B** feel?
  a B is angry.
  b B is happy.
  c B is sorry.
  d B is proud.

Read the conversation and question. Then circle the letter of the correct answer.

Conversation 2

A: How do they feel?

B: They're a bit small. My toes hurt.

A: I can check for a larger size.

B: That would be great.

A: Do you like the color? We have them in red, brown, and blue.

B: I was looking for brown.

A: I'll check.

1 Where are these people?
  a They're at a clothing store.
  b They're at a shoe store.
  c They're at home.
  d They're at a restaurant.

2 Who are these people?
  a **A** is a customer. **B** is a worker.
  b **A** is a mother. **B** is a daughter.
  c **A** and **B** are friends.
  d **A** is a worker. **B** is a customer.

3 What are these people talking about?
  a shoes
  b a skirt
  c pants
  d a shirt

4 What color does **B** want?
  a red
  b brown
  c blue
  d black

Practice 2

Read the conversation and question. Then circle the letter of the correct answer.

Conversation 1

A: Can you go on Saturday?

B: I don't know yet. What time does it start?

A: The doors open at 7:00, but the music doesn't start until 8:00. I want to get there before the band starts playing.

B: OK. I'll ask my mom. How much are the tickets?

A: They're $15 each, but I have an extra ticket, so don't worry about it.

B: Great. Thanks!

1 Who are these people?
  a **A** is a mother. **B** is a daughter.
  b **A** and **B** are friends.
  c **A** and **B** are teachers.
  d **A** is a daughter. **B** is a mother.

2 What are these people talking about?
  a a concert
  b a play
  c a movie
  d a soccer game

3 Does **B** need to buy a ticket?

  a Yes, she needs to buy a ticket.

  b No, she isn't going to go.

  c No, **A** is going to give her a ticket.

  d No, **B** bought a ticket yesterday.

Read the conversation and question. Then circle the letter of the correct answer.

Conversation 2

A: Sorry I'm late!

B: It's almost finished.

A: There were a lot of cars on the road. Who's winning?

B: The score is 5–6.

A: Oh no! How many more minutes?

B: Five.

A: We need to score soon!

1 Where are these people?

  a at a movie

  b in class

  c at a concert

  d at a game

2 Who is winning the game?

  a their team

  b the other team

3 Why was **B** late?

  a There was a party before the game.

  b **B** didn't want to go.

  c **B** was sick.

  d There was a lot of traffic.

Presentation

Making Inferences from Stories

An inference is similar to a guess. We make inferences based on our personal experiences, available information, and our own knowledge about a given topic.

Many times, a writer doesn't give all of the information about a situation. Good readers make inferences about the missing information. Inferences can help us understand a text better and read it faster.

Practice 3

Read the story. Read the question. Then circle the letter of the correct answer.

"Everybody in the car! It's going to be dark soon," cried Mrs. Anderson. Julia, Katie, and Laura ran from behind the house and jumped in the car. Pamela walked slowly to the car. "We can't wait to get to the lake!" Julia and Katie screamed. "This is going to be so much fun!" cried Laura. Pamela gave a big sigh and didn't say anything.

The Anderson family was going on a camping trip. They were going to Bear Lake. The rain had stopped the night before, and it was a beautiful day. When they arrived, the girls got their bags out of the car and started putting up the tents. "The ground is so wet. I don't want to get my new shoes dirty," said Pamela. As Pamela stayed in the car, the other girls looked at one another. "Pamela doesn't do any work," said Julia. "I know! She never helps around the house," said Katie. "Either she doesn't want to get her clothes dirty, or she has to go inside and fix her hair," said Laura. Pamela wasn't like her sisters.

After they set up camp, Julia, Laura, and Katie went to look for wood in the forest. "Let's get lots. I want a big fire," said Julia. Pamela was sitting down at the lake reading a book. "Pamela! Come on! We need to get some wood for the fire tonight," Laura called out. Pamela looked up and said, "No thanks. I don't like fires." The girls looked at one another again. Then Julia said, "OK, but be careful of bears! Remember the name of the lake—Bear Lake!" Pamela looked up. She looked all around her and then said, "Wait for me! I want to go with you!"

The girls looked at Julia. Before Pamela joined them on the path, Laura whispered to Julia, "Are there really bears at this lake?" Julia laughed. "I just want her to help!" The girls laughed, too. When Pamela joined her sisters, they went out into the forest to look for wood.

1 How did Julia, Katie, and Laura feel when they left for Bear Lake?

  a upset

  b excited

  c tired

  d mad

2 How did Pamela feel when they left for Bear Lake?

  a happy

  b sleepy

  c unhappy

  d proud

3 Why does Mrs. Anderson want to leave right away?

  a She wants to go swimming.

  b She doesn't like to drive.

  c She doesn't want to go camping.

  d She wants to get there before the sun sets.

4 Why was the ground wet?

  a It had rained the night before.

  b They were near a lake.

  c It was raining.

  d They spilled their water bottles.

5 How is Pamela different from her sisters?

   a She likes to read.

   b She doesn't have any friends.

   c She doesn't like to get dirty, and she doesn't help.

   d She doesn't like soccer.

6 Why are the sisters looking for wood?

   a They want to scare off the bears.

   b They want a campfire.

   c They want some exercise.

   d They want to set up their tents.

7 Why does Julia say there are bears at the lake?

   a She wants Pamela to look for wood.

   b She wants Pamela to like camping.

   c She wants Pamela to like fires.

   d She wants Pamela to be happy.

8 Why does Pamela help look for wood?

   a She likes to look for wood.

   b She likes to help.

   c She is afraid of bears.

   d She likes fires.

Practice 4

Read the story. Then read the inference. Underline the sentences that support the inference.

"Everybody in the car! It's going to be dark soon," cried Mrs. Anderson. Julia, Katie, and Laura ran from behind the house and jumped in the car. Pamela walked slowly to the car. "We can't wait to get to the lake!" Julia and Katie screamed. "This is going to be so much fun!" cried Laura. Pamela gave a big sigh and didn't say anything.

The Anderson family was going on a camping trip. They were going to Bear Lake. The rain had stopped the night before, and it was a beautiful day. When they arrived, the girls got their bags out of the car and started putting up the tents. "The ground is so wet. I don't want to get my new shoes dirty," said Pamela. As Pamela stayed in the car, the other girls looked at one another. "Pamela doesn't do any work," said Julia. "I know! She never helps around the house," said Katie. "Either she doesn't want to get her clothes dirty, or she has to go inside and fix her hair," said Laura. Pamela wasn't like her sisters.

After they set up camp, Julia, Laura, and Katie went to look for wood in the forest. "Let's get lots. I want a big fire," said Julia. Pamela was sitting down at the lake reading a book. "Pamela! Come on! We need to get some wood for the fire tonight," Laura called out. Pamela looked up and said, "No thanks. I don't like fires." The girls looked at one another again. Then Julia said, "OK, but be careful of bears! Remember the name of the lake—Bear Lake!" Pamela looked up. She looked all around her and then said, "Wait for me! I want to go with you!"

The girls looked at Julia. Before Pamela joined them on the path, Laura whispered to Julia, "Are there really bears at this lake?" Julia laughed. "I just want her to help!" The girls laughed, too. When Pamela joined her sisters, they went out into the forest to look for wood.

1 Inference: Mrs. Anderson wants to leave.

"Everybody in the car! It's going to be dark soon," cried Mrs. Anderson. Julia, Katie, and Laura ran from behind the house and jumped in the car. Pamela walked slowly to the car. "We can't wait to get to the lake," Julia and Katie screamed. "This is going to be so much fun!" cried Laura. Pamela gave a big sigh and didn't say anything.

2 Inference: Pamela doesn't want to go camping.

"Everybody in the car! It's going to be dark soon," cried Mrs. Anderson. Julia, Katie, and Laura ran from behind the house and jumped in the car. Pamela walked slowly to the car. "We can't wait to get to the lake," Julia and Katie screamed. "This is going to be so much fun!" cried Laura. Pamela gave a big sigh and didn't say anything.

3 Inference: Julia, Katie, and Laura are excited about the trip.

"Everybody in the car! It's going to be dark soon," cried Mrs. Anderson. Julia, Katie, and Laura ran from behind the house and jumped in the car. Pamela walked slowly to the car. "We can't wait to get to the lake," Julia and Katie screamed. "This is going to be so much fun!" cried Laura. Pamela gave a big sigh and didn't say anything.

4 Inference: Pamela is afraid of bears.

After they set up camp, Julia, Laura, and Katie went to look for wood in the forest. "Let's get lots. I want a big fire," said Julia. Pamela was sitting down at the lake reading a book. "Pamela! Come on! We need to get some wood for the fire tonight," Laura called out. Pamela looked up and said, "No thanks. I don't like fires." The girls looked at each other again. Then Julia said, "OK, but be careful of bears! Remember the name of the lake—Bear Lake!" Pamela looked up. She looked all around her and then said, "Wait for me! I want to go with you!"

5 Inference: There are no bears at Bear Lake.

The girls looked at Julia. Before Pamela joined them on the path, Laura whispered to Julia, "Are there really bears at this lake?" Julia laughed. "I just want her to help!" The girls laughed, too. When Pamela joined her sisters, they went out into the forest to look for wood.

Comprehension Skills Practice Test

Part 1   Previewing and Predicting

Look at the picture on the page. What is the topic? Circle the letter of the correct answer.

1 This book is about _____ .

   a eating out at restaurants with your family

   b cooking meals with your family

   c reading with your family

2 This book is about _____

   a learning how to garden

   b learning how to cook

   c learning how to clean

Part 2   Previewing and Predicting

Read the chapter title and section heading. Circle the letter of the correct answer.

1 The section is about _____ .
   a traveling by train in Europe
   b modern trains of Europe
   c train accidents
   d how to drive a train

2 The section is about _____ .
   a getting sick
   b washing dishes
   c washing your hands
   d shaking hands

3 The section is about _____ .

  a Italian restaurants

  b using paste

  c making your pasta taste better

  d how to eat pasta

Part 3 Topics and Main Ideas

Read the passage. Is it a paragraph? Circle the letter of the correct answer.

I am going to run in a race next month. I run every day to practice for the race. There are many races around the world. Some races are long. These are called marathons. It is important to have good shoes. Bad shoes can hurt your feet.

1 This is _____ .

  a a paragraph

  b not a paragraph

Vincent van Gogh painted many paintings. He was born in Amsterdam. His paintings were not very popular, and he was not very famous. Today, van Gogh's paintings cost a lot of money. His art is in most of the famous museums around the world.

2 This is _____ .

  a a paragraph

  b not a paragraph

There are many types of dogs. Some are small, and some are large. A husky pulls a sled over snow and ice. My friend has a poodle. It is important to walk your dog every day. Dogs need exercise.

3 This is _____ .

  a a paragraph

  b not a paragraph

Part 4 Topics and Main Ideas

Read the paragraph. Circle the letter of the correct answer.

There are many ways we can help Earth. First, we can recycle. Don't throw glass, paper, and plastic in the trash. Take them to a recycling center. Also, we can reuse things. Don't buy a new water bottle every day. It is better to reuse the same bottle again. These are just a few things we can do to help save our planet.

1 The topic of this paragraph is _____ .
   a how recycling helps Earth
   b how to reuse different products
   c Earth
   d ways to help Earth

New York City is a great place to visit. There is so much to do there. You can go to the theater to see a show. You can go shopping. You can go sightseeing at the Empire State Building or the Statue of Liberty. You can relax in Central Park. New York has it all!

2 The topic of this paragraph is _____ .
   a theater
   b sightseeing
   c shopping
   d New York City

Sleep is very important. Doctors recommend eight hours of sleep every night. Your body and your brain need to rest. One hour before you go to sleep, you should relax with a book or listen to music because sleep is important.

3 The topic of this paragraph is _____ .
   a how to fall asleep
   b the importance of sleep
   c how to read books
   d doctors

Part 5 Topics and Main Ideas

Read the paragraph. Which statement describes the main idea of the paragraph? Circle the letter of the correct answer.

Some schools do not have playtime. The children work all day and do not go outside. Doctors say that playtime is important for children. Their brains need a break. Playtime also helps children learn social skills. Children need to learn how to talk and play with others.

1 a Some schools do not have playtime.
   b Playtime is important for children.
   c We need to give our brains a break.
   d Children need to talk more.

The beach is a nice vacation spot. There are so many things to do at the beach. Many people like to swim and play in the waves. Other people like to look for shells and make sand castles. Some people like to just sit in the sand and read a good book. Whatever you do, the beach is the perfect place for you!

2 **a** How to make a sand castle.
 b The beach is good for swimming and playing.
 c The beach is a good place to take a vacation.
 d Reading and sitting in the sun is fun.

Think about the food you eat. Junk food such as cookies and candy slow your body down. Fast food is cheap and convenient, but it is not good for your body. This kind of food is not healthful, and it makes you feel tired. Think before you eat!

3 **a** Cookies and candy are junk food.
 b Fast food is cheap and convenient.
 c Junk food and fast food are not good for your body.
 d Sleep is important for your body.

Part 6 Scanning

Look at the schedule. Read each question on the next page. Circle the letter of the correct answer.

International Festival
Learning about Countries Around the World
Pan-American Hotel
Saturday, February 22

Time	Event	Room
8:00–9:00	Welcome Breakfast and Check-in	Main Lobby
9:00–10:00	*Once Upon a Time* Listen to famous folk tales from around the world.	Room 201
	Beauty See different forms of art from around the world.	Room 205
10:00–12:00	*Feel the Beat!* Listen to music from around world.	Room 301
	Learn More! Are you interested in studying in another country? Find out how to do it at this session.	Room 207
12:00–1:00	Lunch	Ballroom A
1:00–3:00	*Spin and Twirl* Watch dances from around the world.	Room 202
	At the Movies Choose an international movie to watch. There are five movies to choose from.	Theaters 1–5
3:00–5:00	*Be Creative* Learn how to make a Mexican piñata and an origami paper bird.	Room 302
	Hungry for More Learn how to make three different foods from around the world.	Room 207

1 What is the festival about?

  a dances from around the world

  b countries around the world

  c art from around the world

  d music from around the world

2 If you want to study in another country, which event should you attend?

  a Feel the Beat!

  b Once Upon a Time

  c Learn More!

  d Be Creative

3 What time is the dance event?

  a 1:00–3:00

  b 3:00–5:00

  c 10:00–12:00

  d 1:00–5:00

4 Which class is about cooking?

  a Be Creative

  b Lunch

  c Hungry for More

  d Learn More!

5 Which event is about dancing?

  a Feel the Beat!

  b Spin and Twirl

  c Be Creative

  d Beauty

Part 7 Recognizing Patterns: Time Order

Read the paragraph. Determine the order of each event. Then write the sentences in the correct order on the next page.

When you move into a new house, you want to hang your pictures on the walls. Before you hang them on the wall, look at each room and think what it is for. Then ask yourself "What will I do in each room?" Next, look at all of your pictures. Decide which pictures are best for each room. After you decide which pictures go in each room, look at the walls and decide where to hang the pictures. Finally, hang the pictures on the walls.

Decide where to hang the pictures. You move into a new house.	Hang the pictures on the walls. Decide which pictures are best for each room.	Ask yourself, "What will I do in each room?"	Look at each room and think what it is for.

a _____

b _____

c _____

d _____

e _____

f _____

Part 8   Recognizing Patterns: Listing

Read the paragraph. Find examples related to the main idea of the paragraph. Circle the letter of the correct number of examples in the paragraph.

My favorite thing to do on the weekend is walk. There are many reasons why this is my favorite thing to do. One reason is that it is good for your heart. Another reason is that I can do it outside. I love the outdoors and the fresh air. In addition to the fresh air, you can walk with other people. It is a nice way to spend time with your friends. Another reason is that I can see many areas of the city that you can't see by car.

1 a 3

   b 4

   c 5

   d 6

Karate is a great sport for children. For example, karate teaches children to respect their parents. Karate also helps children focus. In addition, karate helps children with their listening skills. Children who take karate listen well. In addition to these benefits, karate gives children confidence.

2 a 2

   b 3

   c 4

   d 5

Part 9   Recognizing Patterns: Sequence

Read the paragraph. Underline the sentences that have a sequence key word.

Last month, I got my driver's license! It was very exciting. Now I can drive anywhere I want to go. Before I got my license, I had to take the bus to school. I had to wake up early to get to the bus stop. One day, I waited an hour for the bus to come! After that, I decided to study for my driver's test. The next day, I signed up for the class. The class took six months. It wasn't too hard, and I met a lot of nice people. As soon as I got my driver's license, I drove all around town. Now I drive to school every day, and I never take the bus!

Part 10   Making Inferences

Make an inference about the picture. Circle the letter of the correct answer.

1 a proud
   b hungry
   c afraid
   d angry
   e late
   f bored
   g happy
   h sick

2 a angry
   b shy
   c bored
   d sleepy
   e happy
   f hungry
   g proud
   h sick

Part 11   Making Inferences

Read the conversation and questions. Then circle the letter of the correct answer.

A: Hi, Tom. Come on in.

B: You have a nice place.

A: Thanks. I just moved in last month.

B: Wow! Just last month? It looks great!

A: My parents helped a lot.

1 Where are these people?
   a They're at work.
   b They're at **A**'s home.
   c They're at **B**'s home.
   d They're at a store.

2 Who are these people?
   a They are brother and sister.
   b They are friends.
   c **A** is **B**'s mother.
   d **B** is **A**'s father.

3 What are these people talking about?

   a **A**'s new house

   b **B**'s parents

   c **A**'s work

   d school work

4 How does **A**'s house look?

   a The house looks like she just moved in yesterday.

   b The house looks small.

   c The house looks as though she has lived there for more than a month.

   d The house looks dirty.

Part 12　Making Inferences

Read the story. Read each question on the next page. Then choose the correct answer.

The Magic Stone

Long ago, in a village in China, there lived an old farmer and his wife. They were kind to everyone and always gave people food. They worked hard in their fields, but they were getting old. They were not able to gather as much food as they did when they were young. Winter came and they had very little food left in their kitchen. Soon, their food would be gone.

At the same time, an old woman was traveling through their village. It was very cold, and she needed a place to stay. She went to the homes of the other villagers, but they all closed their doors on her. Finally, she came to the old couple's home. She asked for some food and a place to spend the night. The old couple had only one cup of rice left, but they cooked it for the old woman. They watched the old woman eat, and then they helped her into bed. Before she went to sleep, the old woman thanked the couple and gave them a stone. She said, "this is all I have to pay you with." The old couple thanked the woman, and they all went to bed.

The next morning, the old woman was gone. The old couple looked at each other. The man took the stone that the old woman had given them, and he put it in the pot. They went to bed hungry and tired. They thought they would die.

The next morning, the old man smelled fresh rice. He got out of bed and looked in the pot. It was full of rice! He woke up his wife, and they quickly filled their bellies. At the bottom of the pot was the stone the woman had given them. Puzzled, they looked at each other. They didn't understand. They washed the pot and put the stone back inside and went back to sleep. Their hearts and their stomachs were full. They were so thankful to the old woman.

The next morning, the pot was full of rice again. They shared it with their hungry neighbors. They were all able to live through the cold winter. Thanks to the magic stone, they never went hungry again.

1 How would you describe the old couple?

   a kind and selfish

   b generous and kind

   c proud and selfish

   d scared and shy

2 Why did the old couple have so little food?

   a They were lazy.

   b They never shared their food.

   c They were old and not able to gather as much rice as when they were young.

   d Nobody gave them any food.

3 How do we know that the other villagers were not nice to the old woman?

   a They closed their doors on her.

   b They didn't have any doors.

   c They didn't have any food.

   d The old woman was scary.

4 Did the old couple eat with the woman?

   a No, they didn't.

   b Yes, they did.

5 How did the old woman pay the old couple?

   a She paid them with money.

   b She didn't give them anything.

   c She gave them a magic stone.

   d She gave them a pot.

6 What does the following mean: "their hearts and their bellies were full"?

   a Their hearts were sick.

   b They ate well and were happy.

   c They couldn't move.

   d They ate too much.

VOCABULARY BUILDING

Dictionary Work

USING THE DICTIONARY

Presentation

Using the Dictionary
Each bold word in the dictionary is an *entry word*. The listing that follows shows you how to spell and pronounce the word. It also gives the meaning (definition) of the word. Many words have more than one meaning, and a dictionary listing includes all of a word's meanings.

Look at the following sample listing for the word *mad*:

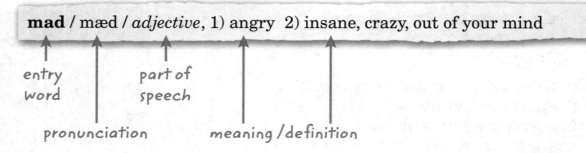

mad / mæd / *adjective*, 1) angry 2) insane, crazy, out of your mind

entry word

pronunciation

part of speech

meaning / definition

Part of speech means the type of word. *Mad* is an adjective. Dictionary listings often include an abbreviation for the parts of speech. Review these abbreviations below:

n = noun
adj = adjective
v = verb
adv = adverb

Practice 1

Read the dictionary entry. What is the underlined part of the entry?

Example:

1 common /ˈkamən/ *adjective*, 1) ordinary 2) general
  a *pronunciation*
  ⓑ *part of speech*
  c *meaning of word*
  d *entry word*

2 unite /yəˈnayt/ *verb* 1) to join together
  a pronunciation
  b part of speech
  c meaning of word
  d entry word

3 numerous /ˈnʊmərəs/ *adjective* 1) many
  a pronunciation
  b part of speech
  c meaning of word
  d entry word

4 basement /'beysmənt/ *noun* 1) part of a building that is underground
- **a** pronunciation
- **b** part of speech
- **c** meaning of word
- **d** entry word

5 sigh /say/ *verb* 1) to let out your breath loudly
- **a** pronunciation
- **b** part of speech
- **c** meaning of word
- **d** entry word

6 trophy /'troʊfi:/ *noun* 1) something you win as a prize or a reward
- **a** pronunciation
- **b** part of speech
- **c** meaning of word
- **d** entry word

7 timid /'tɪməd/ *adjective* 1) shy 2) afraid
- **a** pronunciation
- **b** part of speech
- **c** meaning of word
- **d** entry word

8 designer /dəh'saynər/ *noun* 1) a person who creates something
- **a** pronunciation
- **b** part of speech
- **c** meaning of word
- **d** entry word

Presentation

Using Guide words

Guide words are found at the top of dictionary pages. They show the first and the last words on each page. All of the words on that page are listed alphabetically between these two guide words.

Example:

The word *offer* appears on a page with the two guide words *offend* and *opal*.

Practice 2

Circle the letter of the correct answer.

1 The guide words are *rain* and *ranch*. Which word is not on this dictionary page?
- **a** rattlesnake
- **b** raincoat
- **c** rake
- **d** ramp

2 The guide words are *shadow* and *sheep*. Which word is not on this dictionary page?
- **a** shame
- **b** shake
- **c** shark
- **d** ship

3 The guide words are *part* and *pretty*. Which word is not on this dictionary page?
- **a** port
- **b** pie
- **c** pump
- **d** pet

4 The guide words are *tackle* and *tornado*. Which word is not on this dictionary page?
- **a** train
- **b** team
- **c** tight
- **d** take

5 The guide words are *gardener* and *great*. Which word is not on this dictionary page?
- **a** gear
- **b** gaze
- **c** gauge
- **d** groom

6 The guide words are *feel* and *fuel*. Which word is not on this dictionary page?
- **a** fight
- **b** fox
- **c** fear
- **d** floor

7 The guide words are *abacus* and *ape*. Which word is not on this dictionary page?

   a aardvark

   b apart

   c alligator

   d ace

8 The guide words are *sight* and *soar*. Which word is not on this dictionary page?

   a site

   b similar

   c sleep

   d sickness

PARTS OF SPEECH

Presentation

Parts of Speech

Knowledge of parts of speech helps you know how to use a given word correctly. Review the parts of speech below:

Noun = person, place, thing, or idea

Verb = an action

Adjective = describes something or someone

Adverb = describes a verb (*slowly*), expresses time (*now, then*), manner (*happily, easily*), degree (*less, more, very*), or direction and place (*there, up, down*)

Practice 1

Look at the underlined word. What part of speech is it? Circle the letter of the correct answer.

1 My students <u>arrived</u> late for class.

   a noun

   b adjective

   c verb

   d adverb

2 Tornados are very <u>destructive</u>.

   a noun

   b adjective

   c verb

   d adverb

3 Scientists make many <u>discoveries</u> that help people every day.

   a noun

   b adjective

   c verb

   d adverb

4 The store <u>quickly</u> sold out of all the sale items.

   a noun

   b adjective

   c verb

   d adverb

5 The <u>reflection</u> of the moon was beautiful on the lake last night.

    a noun
    b adjective
    c verb
    d adverb

6 The company will have its meeting <u>next</u> week.

    a noun
    b adjective
    c verb
    d adverb

7 The old woman <u>gazed</u> at the ocean.

    a noun
    b adjective
    c verb
    d adverb

8 There were many <u>friendly</u> people at the party last night.

    a noun
    b adjective
    c verb
    d adverb

Practice 2

Read the words. What are their parts of speech? Put each word in the correct box.

spell	see	boring	carefully
director	beautiful	technology	often
weigh	information	slowly	think
tiny	later	empty	training

verb	adverb	adjective	noun

FINDING THE RIGHT MEANING

Presentation

Words with Multiple Meanings

Many words have more than one meaning. Look at the examples below:

Some words can be both a noun and a verb.

- Here is my <u>report</u>.
- I will <u>report</u> on the news tomorrow.

Some words can be both an adjective and a verb.

- This is the <u>direct</u> route to home.
- Please <u>direct</u> me to the nearest police station.

Some words can be the same part of speech but have different meanings.

- I put some money in the <u>bank</u>.
- He walked slowly along the river <u>bank</u>.

Practice 1

Look at the underlined word. Circle the letter of the correct meaning of the word.

1 The <u>fly</u> was really annoying!
   a to ride in an airplane
   b an insect

2 My office is on the seventh <u>story</u>.
   a a floor of a building
   b something you read

3 The police officers watch the people <u>exit</u> the building.
   a a door that leads you out of a building
   b to leave a building

4 Her skin is usually very <u>fair</u>.
   a light
   b a carnival

5 Many students were <u>present</u> on the day of the exam.
   a a gift
   b to be at a place

6 The students' <u>lounge</u> is a good place to study.
   a to relax
   b a room for relaxing

7 The technical support workers can <u>program</u> your computer for you.

   a to set up

   b a scheduled presentation

8 The <u>content</u> of the book is very interesting.

   a information

   b to be happy

Practice 2

Read the definition in italics. Then read the following sentences and circle the word that has this definition.

1 *a machine that cools a room*

It is very hot in the room today. Unfortunately, our ceiling fan is not working.

You can use these papers to fan yourself, though.

2 *type*

You are very kind to show me your notes from class today.

What kind of test are we having on Friday?

3 *vacation*

Sometimes I am clumsy and trip.

I broke my leg last week, and now I can't go on my trip next week.

4 *to use thoughtlessly*

Generally, Americans waste a lot of food.

They throw their food away, which is a waste.

5 *to see*

I feel bad for my mistake, and my face is red from crying.

I can't face my friends today.

6 *to think highly of something*

I cannot put a value on my friends.

I value my friendships.

7 *surprised*

The electric fence shocked the man.

We were shocked at how much harm it did.

8 *surgery*

The operation went well.

The doctors at that hospital have a well-run operation, and the patient was happy with the results.

Most Common Words

a	because	for	his	made	or	than	to	what
about	been	from	how	make	other	that	took	when
after	but	get	I	me	our	the	two	which
all	by	give	if	most	out	their	up	who
also	came	go	in	my	over	them	us	will
an	can	good	into	new	people	then	use	with
and	come	got	is	no	said	there	want	work
any	could	had	it	not	say	these	was	would
are	day	has	its	now	see	they	way	year
as	did	have	just	of	she	think	we	you
at	do	he	know	on	so	this	well	your
back	even	her	like	one	some	thought	went	
be	first	him	look	only	take	time	were	

Practice 3   The Most Common Words

Write in the missing letters.

1 t ____ o

2 ____ h ____

3 g ____ v ____

4 m ____ k ____

5 ____ ll

6 t ____ e ____

7 ti ____ e

8 wh ____ t

9 y ____ u

10 w ____ r ____

11 ____ nl ____

12 in ____ o

13 com ____

14 an ____

15 be ____ n

16 c ____ n

17 it ____

18 l ____ ____ k

19 ge ____

20 h ____ w

21 ____ ur

22 u ____ e

23 s ____

24 fr ____ m

Practice 4

Write in the missing letters.

1 th ____ ir
2 d ____ y
3 ____ or
4 w ____ u ____ d
5 ____ eo ____ le
6 t ____ ou ____ ____ t
7 m ____ d ____ e
8 mo ____ ____
9 ____ ____ ink
10 ____ ou ____
11 c ____ u ____ ____
12 w ____ n ____

13 w ____ s
14 t ____ an
15 th ____ r ____
16 wi ____ ____
17 ____ ear
18 oth ____ r
19 b ____ cau ____ e
20 a ____ ou ____
21 s ____ ____ d
22 so ____ e
23 w ____ en

Practice 5

Look at the word list below. Find these words from the most common words list and circle them in the grid below.

after	first	like	them
back	good	new	these
came	have	over	went
even	know	take	work

N	E	N	Q	G	O	O	D	L	B
E	M	H	A	V	E	T	R	I	A
W	B	O	V	E	R	H	F	K	C
T	A	F	T	E	R	E	A	E	K
K	D	C	A	M	E	S	K	M	T
N	R	E	P	K	T	E	E	N	V
O	E	C	T	S	F	H	E	W	P
W	Z	V	R	A	T	W	H	O	L
N	L	I	E	T	K	G	Z	R	H
J	F	T	V	N	E	E	Z	K	Q

Practice 6

Write in the missing letters.

1 A: Do y ___ ___ w ___ ___ ___ to go to t ___ ___ movies tonight?

B: I h ___ ___ ___ to wo ___ k tonight.

A: H ___ ___ ab ___ ___ ___ tomorrow?

B: T ___ ___ ___ sounds g ___ ___ ___. What t ___ ___ ___?

A: I th ___ ___ ___ it begins at 9:00 P.M.

2 A: A ___ ___ y ___ ___ ready for dinner?

B: Not yet.

A: I th ___ ___ ___ ___ t you would ___ e hungry.

B: I ate tw ___ sandwiches for lunch.

3 A: Excuse m ___, whi ___ ___ building is t ___ ___ library?

B: I thi ___ ___ it's ov ___ ___ the ___ ___.

A: Thank you. Also, a ___ ___ there a ___ ___ restaurants around here?

B: What kind o ___ food do you w ___ ___ ___?

A: A ___ ___ kind. I ___ ___ very hungry.

Word Parts

PREFIXES

> ### Presentation
>
> **Prefixes**
>
> Some words have different parts. If you know what the parts mean, then you can understand the words better.
>
> A prefix is one or more letters added before a root word to modify its meaning.
>
> **Example:** <u>un</u>healthy (not healthy)
>
> Look at the following list of common prefixes and their meanings:
>
> | | | |
> |---|---|---|
> | un = not | im = not | re = again |
> | dis = not | pre = before | mis = wrong |
> | non = not | post = after | under = under |

Practice 1

Look at the list of words. What prefix do they all share? Circle the prefix and its meaning.

1

unfair	unhappy	unusual	unkind

Prefix: un, dis, mis, pre, under, re, non
Meaning: under, not, wrong, before, again

2

mistake	misuse	misunderstand	mishandle

Prefix: un, dis, mis, pre, under, re, non
Meaning: under, not, wrong, before, again

3

nonsmoker	nonfiction	nonviolent	nonsense

Prefix: un, dis, mis, pre, under, re, non
Meaning: under, not, wrong, before, again

4

disregard	disassemble	disappear	dislike

Prefix: un, dis, mis, pre, under, re, non
Meaning: under, not, wrong, before, again

5

preview	preread	preconceive	prepay

Prefix: un, dis, mis, pre, under, re, non
Meaning: under, not, wrong, before, again

6

review	reread	retake	revisit

Prefix: un, dis, mis, pre, under, re, non
Meaning: under, not, wrong, before, again

Practice 2

Read the sentences. Circle the letter of the correct answer.

1 I would like to hear the story again. Could you _____ it, please?
   a retell   **b** tell

2 My mother and I often argue. We _____ on many issues.
   a disagree   **b** agree

3 My sister likes to be prepared for class. She _____ the chapter before the teacher teaches it.
   a reviews   **b** previews

4 I don't study for my English tests very often. I often _____ words on the test.
   a spell   **b** misspell

5 My mom doesn't like cell phones at dinner. She _____ of phone calls at the table.
   a disapproves   **b** approves

6 My sister hurt her leg. She is _____ to walk.
   a unable   **b** able

7 I _____ the directions to the party. We were lost for two hours!
   a understood   **b** misunderstood

8 My father likes history. He reads a lot of _____ books.
   a nonfiction   **b** fiction

Practice 3

Read the paragraph. Circle the correct words.

1 Circle the words with the prefix *un*.

I am unhappy with my new roommate. She is very unfriendly. She doesn't say a word to me. I feel very uncomfortable around her. She thinks it's unnecessary to get to know each other.

2 Circle the words with the prefix *non*.

I am looking for a new partner in class. My partner talks nonstop. She doesn't say anything important. She just talks nonsense. She also smells of smoke. The smell makes me sick. I need a partner that is a nonsmoker.

3 Circle the words with the prefix *pre*.

The new movie is coming out next week. I saw the preview and I think it looks really good. Many people are making plans to go. My friend suggested we should preorder the tickets for next week. I am going to prepay for a ticket, so I can be sure to go.

4 Circle the words with the prefix *mis*.

The new student isn't doing very well in class. She misunderstands the directions. She also misuses some English words. She can't spell very well. She misspells all the time.

SUFFIXES

> **Presentation**
>
> **Suffixes**
>
> Some words have different parts. If you know what the parts mean, then you can understand the words better.
>
> A suffix is one or more letters added after a root word to modify its meaning.
>
> > **Example:** worke<u>r</u> (a person or thing that works)
>
> A suffix changes the meaning and often the part of speech of a word.
>
> > **Examples:** *Work* is a verb, but *worker* is a noun. *Loud* is an adjective, but *loudly* is an adverb. *Friend* is a noun, but *friendly* is an adjective.
>
> Sometimes, the spelling of the root word changes when you add a suffix.
>
> > **Example:** *happy > happiness*

Practice 1

Look at the words. Circle the correct parts of speech.

1 work > worker

Part of speech for the root word: verb, adverb, adjective

Part of speech for the word with suffix: noun, verb, adverb, adjective

2 light > lightly

Part of speech for the root word: verb, adverb, adjective

Part of speech for the word with suffix: noun, verb, adverb, adjective

3 sleepy > sleepiness

Part of speech for the root word: verb, adverb, adjective

Part of speech for the word with suffix: noun, verb, adverb, adjective

4 thank > thankful

Part of speech for the root word: noun, verb, adjective

Part of speech for the word with suffix: noun, verb, adverb, adjective

5 sweet > sweetest

Part of speech for the root word: verb, adverb, adjective

Part of speech for the word with suffix: noun, verb, adverb, adjective

6 friend > friendless

Part of speech for the root word: noun, adverb, adjective

Part of speech for the word with suffix: noun, verb, adverb, adjective

Practice 2

Read the sentences. Circle the letter of the correct answer.

1 Don't drink that water! It's _____ .
   a dirt
   b dirty

2 The man fixed my computer. He was very _____ .
   a helpful
   b help

3 That is a glass plate. Please put it _____ on the table.
   a carefully
   b careful

4 My mom is a _____ . She works with children.
   a teach
   b teacher

5 My sister breaks dishes all the time. She _____ handles them.
   a careless
   b carelessly

6 My grandfather loved boats. He was an excellent _____ .
   a sail
   b sailor

7 The movie was boring. It was a bit _____ for me.

    a child

    b childish

8 Your daughter's paintings are beautiful. She is a very good _____ .

    a artist

    b art

Practice 3

Circle the letter of the correct answer.

1 Which suffix can be added to the root word *nature*?

    a er

    b al

    c or

    d ful

2 Which suffix can be added to the root word *self*?

    a ish

    b for

    c er

    d al

3 Which suffix can be added to the root word *cloud*?

    a ish

    b ful

    c al

    d y

4 Which suffix can be added to the root word *art*?

    a er

    b or

    c ist

    d ish

5 Which suffix can be added to the root word *drive*?

    a or

    b less

    c er

    d full

6 Which suffix can be added on to the root word *care*?

    a less

    b ist

    c er

    d all

7 Which suffix can be added to the root word *emotion*?

    a y

    b ful

    c or

    d al

8 Which suffix can be added on to the root word *popular*?

    a ity

    b ful

    c er

    d al

WORD FORMS AND FAMILIES

Presentation

Word Forms and Families

A word family is a group of words with the same root word. They are all part of the same family of meaning, but they have different parts of speech.

Look at the examples below:

Root word: quick	Root word: strong
quick = adjective	strong = adjective
quickness = noun	strength = noun
quickly = adverb	strengthen = verb
quicken = verb	strongly = adverb

Practice 1

Draw lines to match the words with the correct parts of speech.

1 a beautiful   adjective
  b beauty   noun
  c beautifully   adverb

2 a help   adjective
  b helpful   noun
  c helplessly   adverb

3 a energetically   adverb
  b energy   verb
  c energize   noun

4 a attract   adjective
  b attractive   noun
  c attraction   verb

5 a soft   noun
  b softness   adverb
  c softly   adjective

6 a compare   adverb
  b comparison   verb
  c comparatively   noun

7 a advise   noun
  b advisor   adjective
  c advisable   verb

8 a notice   adverb
  b noticeable   adjective
  c noticeably   verb

Practice 2

Read the words. What are their parts of speech? Put each word in the correct box.

inventive	preference	succeed	successful
preferable	discover	creative	success
informative	reaction	inform	discovery
invention	information	create	prefer
creation	react	invent	

noun	verb	adjective

Presentation

Word Forms and Families

Some words have the same spelling and pronunciation but have different meanings and can be different parts of speech. These words are called homonyms.

Examples:

The score of the soccer game is 3 to 2.

I score many points.

Practice 3

Circle the letter of the correct part of speech.

1 The <u>report</u> is due tomorrow.
  a noun
  b verb

2 Please <u>report</u> to the office immediately.
  a noun
  b verb

3 We had a nice <u>visit</u> with my family.
  a noun
  b verb

4 They <u>visit</u> their grandparents every summer.
  a noun
  b verb

5 The <u>shop</u> closes at 4 p.m. today.
  a noun
  b verb

6 Do you <u>shop</u> at that store often?
  a noun
  b verb

7 The president <u>rules</u> the company well.
  a noun
  b verb

8 She likes to follow the <u>rules</u> every time.
  a noun
  b verb

9 The landlord <u>objects</u> to having pets in the apartment.
  a noun
  b verb

10 The museum has a lot of valuable <u>objects</u>.
  a noun
  b verb

11 That dog is the leader of the <u>pack</u>.
  a noun
  b verb

12 I have to <u>pack</u> my clothes for the trip.
  a noun
  b verb

13 That machine <u>projects</u> the movie onto the wall.
  a noun
  b verb

14 The company has a lot of <u>projects</u> in February.
  a noun
  b verb

Practice 4

Read the sentences. Circle the letter of the correct answer.

1 Don't text while driving. It is _____ .

   a dangerous   **b** danger

2 The doctor is a _____ in that disease.

   a special   **b** specialist

3 I like to go to _____ areas on my hikes.

   a natural   **b** nature

4 That snake is _____ . Be careful!

   a poisonous   **b** poison

5 I'm sorry you're in debt, but you need to take more _____ .

   a responsible   **b** responsibility

6 I _____ that it will snow a lot this winter.

   a predict   **b** prediction

7 My younger sister is afraid of _____ .

   a stormy   **b** storms

8 Work on the new school is almost _____ .

   a completion   **b** complete

Guessing Meaning from Context

WHAT IS CONTEXT?

> **Presentation**
>
> **What Is Context?**
> When reading, it is not necessary to understand every word in a sentence or group of sentences. Often, you can understand or even guess the meaning of a word or phrase from context. The words or sentences around a word or phrase are the context. From the context, you can learn the following:
>
> - the part of speech of a word
> - the general meaning of a word or phrase

Practice 1

Read the sentences. Circle the part that best explains the underlined word or phrase.

1 She <u>seldom</u> sees her grandparents. She only goes to their house once a month.

2 I don't like to study at my friend's house. Her little brother is a <u>nuisance</u>. He bothers us while we are studying.

3 The new movie is very <u>humorous</u>. We laughed the entire time! I really recommend it.

4 The students like to <u>hang out</u> in that coffee shop. They sit there for hours. Most of the students relax, but some study.

5 Last year, I had a lot of <u>misfortune</u> in my life. Everywhere I went, there was bad luck. I hope this year will be better!

6 The television is <u>complicated</u> to set up. I had a very difficult time with it. I'm going to ask my neighbor to help me.

Practice 2

Read the sentences. What is the meaning of the underlined word? Circle the letter of the correct answer.

1 <u>Etiquette</u> is not important to many parents today. Good manners are not a priority in raising their children, unfortunately.

   a unfortunately   **b** good manners   **c** priority

2 The soccer team was so <u>boisterous</u> after the game. We couldn't hear the announcement because the players were so loud!

   a loud   **b** announcement   **c** couldn't hear

3 The <u>primate</u> house at the zoo opens on Sunday. There will be six different kinds of apes.

   a zoo   **b** apes   **c** kind

4 In certain states, it is illegal to talk on a cell phone and drive at the same time. The safest thing to do is to <u>pull over</u>. Get off the road and then make your phone call.

   a get off the road   **b** make a phone call   **c** illegal

5 The flu seems to be very bad this year. People who get it are <u>miserable</u>. They feel very bad that they have to stay in bed all day long.

   a in bed   **b** stay   **c** very bad

6 The teacher <u>observes</u> her students' progress every day. She watches them and then decides what material is best for them.

   a decides   **b** watches   **c** progress

7 It is difficult to <u>determine</u> the family's needs. One way to find out is to ask the neighbors.

   a find out   **b** forget   **c** ask

GUESSING THE MEANING OF WORDS

Presentation

Guess the Missing Word

When reading, it is not necessary to understand every word in a sentence or group of sentences. Often, you can understand or even guess the meaning of a word or phrase from context. The words or sentences around a word or phrase are the context. From the context, you can learn the following:

- the part of speech of a word
- the general meaning of a word or phrase

Practice 1

Read the sentences. What is the part of speech of the missing word? Circle the letter of the correct answer.

1 The school opened two years ago. There are 120 _____ and 10 teachers. The parents appreciate the attention that their children receive.

   a verb

   b noun

   c adjective

   d adverb

2 The scientist _____ the sick animals at the aquarium. He has an important job.

   a verb

   b noun

   c adjective

   d adverb

3 Sarah moved into a new apartment. It is _____ and beautiful. She likes her new place.

   a verb

   b noun

   c adjective

   d adverb

4 The surgery went well. The patient walks very _____ , but he is making progress.

   a verb

   b noun

   c adjective

   d adverb

5 The family stayed at the mountain house last year. Their _____ is on top of Black Mountain.

   a verb

   b noun

   c adjective

   d adverb

6 The new waiter is _____ . He is polite to the customers and works hard.

   a verb

   b noun

   c adjective

   d adverb

7 Sam _____ comes to school on time, but, lately, he has been arriving late.

   a verb

   b noun

   c adjective

   d adverb

8 My doctor told me to _____ every day. It is good for my heart.

   a verb

   b noun

   c adjective

   d adverb

Practice 2

Read the sentences. What is the part of speech of the missing word? Circle the letter of the correct answer.

1 The people of Spain _____ dinner late in the evening.

   a verb

   b noun

   c adjective

   d adverb

2 Huskies are _____ dogs. They are known for pulling dog sleds.

   a verb

   b noun

   c adjective

   d adverb

3 The snow is _____ melting due to the warm weather. Spring will come soon.

   a verb

   b noun

   c adjective

   d adverb

4 Many people from Germany came to the United States and settled in the northern states. They _____ bakeries and food markets.

   a verb

   b noun

   c adjective

   d adverb

5 That _____ has many kinds of plants. They sell their plants to the flower markets in town.

   a verb

   b noun

   c adjective

   d adverb

6 A cheetah runs very _____ . It is one of the fastest animals on Earth.

   a verb

   b noun

   c adjective

   d adverb

7 Leonardo da Vinci's *Mona Lisa* is a _____ painting. It is one of the most recognized paintings in the world.

   a verb

   b noun

   c adjective

   d adverb

8 That _____ is very difficult. The professor is very strict, and the content is complicated.

   a verb

   b noun

   c adjective

   d adverb

Practice 3

Read the passage. What are the parts of speech of the missing words? Circle the correct answers.

Nowadays, many people (verb/noun/adjective) to go geocaching. There are two types of people involved in this (adverb/noun/adjective). First, there are the people who hide a box. They write clues for other people to find their (verb/adjective/noun) .

The other people are the seekers. The seekers (adverb/noun/verb) the clues to find the boxes. Once they find a box, they can write their name or put a stamp on the paper inside the box. This shows other people that someone (verb/adjective/adverb) it before them. Some of the boxes have (adjective/noun/adverb) treasures inside. If you find the box, you get to take one.

There are millions of geocache boxes all around the (noun/verb/adjective). Some people travel to other states and even other countries to find these boxes. Many boxes are in (noun/adverb/adjective) places around the world. It can be a great way to see the world!

Practice 4

Read the sentences. What are the missing words? Circle the correct answers.

Nowadays, many people (like/path/short) to go geocaching. There are two types of people involved in this (slowly/hobby/beautiful). First, there are the people who hide a box. They write clues for other people to find their (hike/long/boxes) .

The other people are the seekers. The seekers (carefully/pencil/follow) the clues to find the boxes. Once they find a box, they can write their name or put a stamp on the paper inside the box. This shows other people that someone (found/fast/later) it before them. Some of the boxes have (small/weather/slowly) treasures inside. If you find the box, you get to take one.

There are millions of geocache boxes all around the (world/seek/difficult). Some people travel to other states and even other countries to find these boxes. Many boxes are in (house/later/interesting) places around the world. It can be a great way to see the world!

Presentation

Guess the Meaning of Words

When reading, it is not necessary to understand every word in a sentence or group of sentences. Often, you can understand or even guess the meaning of a word or phrase from context. The words or sentences around a word or phrase are the context. From the context, you can learn the following:

- the part of speech of a word
- the general meaning of a word or phrase

Practice 5

Read the sentences. What is the meaning of the underlined word? Circle the letter of the correct answer.

1 My classmate talks a lot during class. I try to <u>ignore</u> her. I don't listen to her and try hard to listen only to the teacher.

   a like

   b not pay attention to

   c talk to

   d become friends

2 Spring came early this year. The flowers usually <u>bloom</u> in May, but they have already appeared!

   a come out

   b die

   c plant

   d dig

3 Mr. Johnson is moving to Texas. Our class said <u>farewell</u> to him yesterday. It was hard to see him go.

   a hello

   b get better

   c goodbye

   d How are you?

4 My parents like their friends Jim and Mary Nelson. They always <u>run into</u> them at the coffee shop. They never make plans to see one another, but they enjoy the surprise encounters.

   a make a plan to see someone

   b fall into someone

   c crash into someone

   d see someone unexpectedly

5 Police officers <u>investigate</u> any suspicious behavior. They look into anything that appears strange or out of the ordinary.

   a check out

   b call

   c find

   d see

6 That horse is very <u>clever</u>. He is able to escape his stable every day.

   a smart

   b sweet

   c tall

   d funny

Practice 6

Read the sentences. What is the meaning of the underlined word? Circle the letter of the correct answer.

1 I bought some balloons for the party. We need to <u>inflate</u> them before everyone gets here. Can you help me?

   a throw away

   b fill with air

   c hang

   d use

2 A lot of <u>elderly</u> people go to that restaurant. They give a discount to people over 65 years of age. My grandparents like to eat there.

    a old

    b young

    c intelligent

    d poor

3 I recommend that you <u>hail</u> a taxi. It will take you straight to the building, and it will be a lot faster than the bus.

    a drive

    b stop

    c signal to stop

    d sit on top of

4 She is young, but she's very <u>mature</u> for her age. She focuses on her work and is very responsible.

    a smart

    b short

    c advanced

    d talkative

5 I heard you got a parking ticket last week. The <u>maximum</u> that students have to pay is $20. Other people have to pay $50!

    a least

    b most

    c ticket

    d bill

6 It was strange to see an owl in the tree during the day. Owls are <u>nocturnal</u> animals. They usually only come out at night.

    a friendly

    b sleepy

    c shy

    d active at night

How Words Work Together

PHRASES

Presentation

Common Types of Phrases

There are some words that are often used together. This group of words is called a phrase. Knowing common phrases will help you understand what you read.

Here are some common types of phrases:

verb + noun: I need to <u>do homework</u> tonight.

verb + preposition (phrasal verb): Please <u>hang up</u> your coat in the closet.

prepositional phrases: The coffee shop is <u>in front of</u> the school.

adverbial phrases: The train always arrives <u>on time</u>.

Practice 1

Match each phrase with its meaning. Draw lines to make a match.

1 a make up your mind   call someone
  b make a call   put sheets on a bed
  c make sure   try hard
  d make an effort   decide
  e make a bed   be certain

2 a put away   stop a fire from burning
  b put down   put something in the place where it is usually kept
  c put off   wait to do something
  d put out   wear something on your body
  e put on   say something bad about someone or something
  f put up with   tolerate someone or something

3 a take out   look or act like someone
  b take off   take control
  c take after   begin a new activity
  d take over   take someone on a date
  e take up   remove something from your body

Practice 2

Circle the letter of the phrase that correctly completes the sentence.

1 Sam waited by the phone _____ . He didn't want to miss the call from his grandmother.

   a all day

   b at last

   c for now

   d on time

   e right away

   f all the time

   g for example

2 She wasn't feeling well this morning. _____ , she is staying home from school. She'll see how she feels later today.

   a All day

   b At last

   c For now

   d On time

   e Right away

   f All the time

   g For example

3 Mark was a bit shy at the party. _____ , Tom came up to him, and they talked all night.

   a All day

   b For a while

   c On time

   d Right away

   e All the time

   f For example

4 The teacher talks about technology _____ . Every day, she shows us how we can use technology in our projects.

   a at last

   b for now

   c on time

   d right away

   e all the time

   f for example

5 You will see many kinds of wildlife in the forest. _____ , there are bears, wolves, and deer.

   a All day

   b At last

   c For now

   d On time

   e For a while

   f For example

6 They traveled a long way. _____ , they reached their destination. It was a tiring trip.

   a All day

   b At last

   c For now

   d On time

   e For a while

   f For example

7 We waited for a long time at the bus stop. This was unusual. The bus was usually _____ .

   a all day

   b at last

   c for now

   d on time

   e all the time

   f for example

8 Nancy lived in Texas _____ . After that, she moved to New York.

   a all day

   b at last

   c on time

   d for a while

   e right away

   f for example

Practice 3

Read the sentences. What is the missing phrase? Circle the letter of the correct answer.

1 Joe wants to _____ Mary next Saturday night. They are going to go to the movies.

  a take out
  b take after
  c take over

2 It is not nice to _____ your sister. She is a part of your family, and you shouldn't say bad things about her.

  a put on
  b put down
  c put off

3 The teacher wasn't sure which day the test was going to be. Yesterday, she _____ to have the test next week.

  a made up her mind
  b made a call
  c made sure

4 My grandparents are going to _____ golf. They have their first lesson next week.

  a take out
  b take off
  c take up

5 Kate usually _____ her little sisters. Today, though, she lost her patience and got angry with them.

  a puts up with
  b puts out
  c puts off

6 The teacher always _____ to have a fun activity every day in class. She tries hard to make learning enjoyable.

  a makes her bed
  b makes a call
  c makes an effort

Practice 4

Write in a phrase from the box to correctly complete the sentence. Pay attention to spelling. Use the correct verb form.

cheer up	get off	give up	pick out
cross out	get over	lie down	
drop off	get up	pass out	

1 The boys _____ the bus at the last stop. They walk home together.

2 Madelyn likes to _____ her own ice cream. She looks at all of the flavors and then chooses the one she wants.

3 My parents told me to never _____ . They said that I should always keep trying.

4 These answers are all wrong. Please _____ your answers and reread the questions.

5 You have to _____ the papers at the office.

6 Let's go _____ Mrs. Hanson. She is sad about her dog.

7 Neil's job is to _____ the papers in school. He likes to help the teacher.

8 My dog likes to sleep in my room. He _____ beside my bed every night.

9 The family _____ at 6:30 every morning. They all eat together and then leave for school and work.

10 It takes a long time to _____ this sickness. All you can do is rest.

Practice 5

Read the sentences. Circle the letter of the correct answer.

1 On the farm, everyone _____ early in the morning. The day begins around 5:00 A.M.

   a gets up

   b lies down

   c gets off

2 Let's _____ Sally. Ice cream always makes her happy.

   a give up

   b pick out

   c cheer up

3 The teacher _____ the test. The students sat quietly and answered the questions.

   a passed out

   b crossed out

   c got up

4 Megan drives everyone home after school. First, she _____ Joe and Kelly, and then she drives home.

   a gives up

   b drops off

   c lies down

5 The patients _____ their colds quickly. They rested all day and felt much better in the morning.

   a crossed out

   b got over

   c cheered up

6 The team loses a lot of games, but they never _____ . They keep trying to win.

   a give up

   b lie down

   c get up

7 The girls _____ their clothes before school. They look at the weather and decide which clothing is best for the day.

   a drop off

   b get over

   c pick out

8 Her name was spelled incorrectly. She _____ her name and wrote it correctly.

   a picked out

   b crossed out

   c passed out

PARTS OF SENTENCES

Presentation

Key Parts of Sentences

The most important parts of a sentence are the subject and the verb. The subject tells who or what the sentence is about. The verb tells what the subject does or gives information about the subject.

Example:

<u>Sam</u> [subject] <u>rides</u> [verb] his bicycle to school.

Sam is the subject. This sentence is about Sam. *Rides* is the verb. The verb tells us what Sam does.

Practice 1

Circle the subject of each sentence.

1 Yoko is from Japan.

2 She goes to school in the United States.

3 Her roommate is from Mexico.

4 They speak to each other in English.

5 Many international students study at the school.

6 Yoko's family visits her in the summer.

7 They travel around the United States.

8 Many Japanese tourists visit the United States each year.

Practice 2

Circle the verb in each sentence.

1 Yoko is from Japan.

2 She goes to school in the United States.

3 Her roommate is from Mexico.

4 They speak to each other in English.

5 Many international students study at the school.

6 Yoko's family visits her in the summer.

7 They travel around the United States.

8 Many Japanese tourists visit the United States each year.

PERSONAL PRONOUNS AND POSSESSIVE ADJECTIVES

Personal Pronouns and Possessive Adjectives

Pronouns are words that replace nouns or noun phrases in a sentence. Pronouns refer to people or things already identified in the sentence or paragraph. There are many types of pronouns.

Subject pronouns can be the subject of a sentence.

Example:

Mary likes to bake cookies. She bakes cookies every day.

Object pronouns can be the object of a verb or preposition.

Example:

Mary likes to bake cookies. She bakes <u>them</u> every day.

Possessive adjectives show that something belongs to someone or something.

Example:

She always gives them to <u>her</u> friends and neighbors.

Practice 1

Circle the pronoun or adjective that correctly completes each sentence.

1 Ana is a nurse at the hospital. (She/Her/He) helps patients. (She/Her/He) gives (her/their/them) medicine.

2 David bought a dog last week. (She/He/It) named (them/its/it) Sierra. David really likes Sierra, but (her/his/its) cat is not happy!

3 Connor and Calvin are friends. (Them/Their/They) met each other last year, and (them/their/they) never stopped talking in class. (Them/Their/They) teacher didn't want (them/their/they) to sit next to each other.

4 Katie hurt (his/her/it) arm yesterday. (She/He/It) broke her arm playing tennis. (Her/He/It) needs to be in a cast for six weeks.

5 I really like my new car. (He/She/It) is very fast, and (my/his/its) color is a beautiful blue. (It/I/She) drive it everywhere!

6 You need to get a haircut before (my/your/you) interview. I recommend you get (her/me/it) at the new salon. The hair stylist there is really good. (It/She/They) does a thorough job.

Practice 2

Complete the paragraph with the correct pronouns and adjectives.

1 Marta and her brother Miguel are from Spain. _____ came to the United

States last year. In Spain, _____ parents have a company.

_____ is small. Marta and Miguel want to help _____ with the

company, so they are going to learn English.

2 Marta and Miguel have a younger sister, Maria. _____ is only ten years

old. _____ misses _____ brother and sister very much, and

_____ wants to live in the United States, too. _____ parents

tell _____ that _____ is too young.

3 Marta has a boyfriend in Spain. _____ name is Javier. _____

wants to marry Marta. _____ gave her a necklace before she left. She

really likes _____ color. She wears _____ every day and

thinks of Javier.

Vocabulary Building Practice Test

Part 1   Using a Dictionary

Read the dictionary entry. Read the question. Circle the letter of the correct answer.

1 miniscule /ˈmɪnəskyul/ *adjective,* 1) <u>very small</u>

What is the underlined part of the entry?

a pronunciation
b part of speech
c meaning of word
d entry word

2 <u>hostess</u> /ˈhoʊstəs/ *noun,* 1) the woman who invited the guests and organized a party

What is the underlined part of the entry?

a pronunciation
b part of speech
c meaning of word
d entry word

3 firm /fɚm/ *noun,* 1) <u>a business or small company</u>

What is the underlined part of the entry?

a pronunciation
b part of speech
c meaning of word
d entry word

4 The guidewords are *muffin* and *must.* Which word is not on this dictionary page?

a mustache
b mug
c music
d multiple

5 The guidewords are *occur* and *official.* Which word is not on this dictionary page?

a odd
b officer
c off
d occupy

6 The deer <u>ran</u> through the forest.

What is the part of speech of the underlined word?

a noun
b adjective
c verb
d adverb

7 The paper is very *thin*.

What is the part of speech of the underlined word?

a noun

b adjective

c verb

d adverb

8 There was a lot of <u>information</u>.

What is the part of speech of the underlined word?

a noun

b adjective

c verb

d adverb

Part 2   Using a Dictionary

Read the questions. Then circle the correct words in the sentences.

1 Which word in the following sentence means *relax*?
Read the rest of that page and then you can rest.

2 Which word in the following sentences means a *show*?
My children are going to be in a play next month. They really like to play with costumes.

Part 3   Word Parts: Prefixes

Look at the list of words. What prefix do they all share? Circle the prefix and its meaning.

1 preheat, precook, preview, preschool

Prefix: dis, mis, non, pre, re, un, under

Meaning: again, before, not, under, wrong

2 unhappy, unwell, undone, unbelievable

Prefix: dis, mis, non, pre, re, un, under

Meaning: again, before, not, under, wrong

3 disagree, disrespect, disobey, disapprove

Prefix: dis, mis, non, pre, re, un, under

Meaning: again, before, not, under, wrong

4 nonverbal, nonsense, nonsmoking, nonstop

Prefix: dis, mis, non, pre, re, un, under

Meaning: again, before, not, under, wrong

Part 4   Word Parts: Suffixes

Read the sentences. Circle the letter of the correct answers.

1 The cat was so _____ . He slept on the couch all day.
   a sleep
   b sleepy

2 I like that restaurant. The waiters are very _____ .
   a friend
   b friendly

3 There were many _____ at school today.
   a visit
   b visitors

4 The children are very _____ for the candy.
   a thank
   b thankful

Part 5   Word Forms and Families

Draw lines to match the words with the correct parts of speech.

1 a sad   adverb
   b sadness   adjective
   c sadly   noun

2 a dangerous   noun
   b danger   adjective
   c dangerously   adverb

Part 6   Guessing Meaning from Context

Read the sentences. Circle the word or phrase that best explains the underlined word or phrase.

1 We cleaned our house yesterday. I <u>polished</u> the furniture. I made it bright and shiny again.

2 Do you like my new <u>outfit</u>? I bought the clothes at the new store downtown.

3 The play was so <u>dramatic</u>. It was a very exciting play to watch.

4 My little sister <u>snoops around</u> my room a lot. She is always secretly looking through my things. She is very annoying.

Part 7   Guessing Meaning from Context

Read the sentences. What is the part of speech of the missing word? Circle the letter of the correct answer.

1 The old _____ was destroyed in the accident.
- **a** verb
- **b** noun
- **c** adjective
- **d** adverb

2 The old man _____ his garden until he was eighty-five years old.
- **a** verb
- **b** noun
- **c** adjective
- **d** adverb

3 The new girl was very _____. We all liked her immediately.
- **a** verb
- **b** noun
- **c** adjective
- **d** adverb

4 The dogs barked _____ all night long.
- **a** verb
- **b** noun
- **c** adjective
- **d** adverb

Part 8   How Words Work Together

Draw lines to match each phrase with its meaning.

1
- **a** get on   take a vacation
- **b** get in   step onto a vehicle (bicycle, train, bus)
- **c** get along with   wake up
- **d** get away   step into a vehicle (car)
- **e** get up   like other people

2
- **a** look for   be careful
- **b** look forward to   respect someone
- **c** look out   check something
- **d** look over   be excited about something
- **e** look up   try to find something
- **f** look up to   find information in a book

Part 9   How Words Work Together

Write a phrase from the box to correctly complete each sentence.

make a mistake	put on	in back of
do the dishes	at night	

1 It is important to make an effort in language class. Don't worry if you _____ . You don't need to be embarrassed.

2 The weather is cold and rainy today. Remember to _____ a coat and a warm hat.

3 I usually study _____ . The house is quiet, and I can focus on my work.

4 The new coffee shop is _____ the restaurant.

5 My brother and I share the jobs around the house. I _____ and he cleans the bathrooms.

Part 10   How Words Work Together

Circle the pronoun that correctly completes each sentence.

1 Sam lives in a nice apartment building. (It/Its/They) has a pool. (He/Him/She) uses (it/them/they) every day.

2 Our new neighbors are very nice. (Their/Them/They) daughter's name is Sophia. (He/Her/She) is really cute.

3 (Our/Them/We) new teacher is very strict. (He/Her/Him) gives (they/us/we) a lot of homework. I don't like (he/her/him).

4 Carol and Maria are best friends. (She/They/We) have known each other since (her/our/their) school days.

5 (I/My/You) sister's name is Claudia. She and I are very close. (I/We/You) do everything together.

THINKING IN ENGLISH

Thinking in English Practice

Practice 1

Circle the letter of the word that correctly completes the sentence.

1 Last week, Kristen went to a party at her friend's house. There were many people there. They danced and played _____ all night long.

   a chairs

   b music

   c presents

   d decorations

2 We saw many animals at the zoo yesterday. There were giraffes, elephants, and lions. We did not see the _____ . They were not in their cages.

   a people

   b food

   c doctors

   d monkeys

3 William got hurt in the soccer game. He left the game _____ to go to the hospital. The team went to see him after the game.

   a early

   b Monday

   c late

   d ball

4 My back hurts. Can you help me get out of this _____ ? I can't do it myself.

   a beds

   b table

   c chair

   d floor

5 We usually eat dinner very late. We wait for everyone to get home from work and school. Then, after we talk for a while, we eat around _____ .

   a late

   b 8:00 P.M.

   c 8:00 A.M.

   d dinner

6 Martin and Maria eat lunch after class every day. They like all kinds of food. Today, they are going to eat at the _____ restaurant.

   a Japanese

   b Japan

   c food

   d table

7 Yuki is a student. She studies all day and all evening. Every afternoon, she studies at the library. After dinner, she studies at home because the library is closed _____ .

   a at lunch time

   b in the evenings

   c in the mornings

   d on Sundays

8 Everyone in Tom's family is very tall. Tom's mother and father are very tall. Tom's brother is tall. Even Tom's little sister is tall. Tom is not tall. He is _____ .

   a old

   b young

   c small

   d short

Practice 2

Circle the letter of the word that correctly completes the sentence.

1 There was an accident in front of my house yesterday. A car hit a man on a bicycle. Luckily, the man was not _____ .

   a sick

   b dangerous

   c hurt

   d tall

2 Laura cleans her house on Saturdays. First, she begins with the kitchen, and then she cleans the bathrooms. After the bathrooms, she cleans the _____ .

   a car

   b living room

   c house

   d telephone

3 The winter is beautiful in this part of the country. The air is fresh, and there is a lot of snow. It's not very cold, so it is a good time of year to be _____ .

  a outside
  b inside
  c awake
  d young

4 Harry is an office manager. He works many hours each day. There is nobody to help him do the work. He is angry that he doesn't make more _____ .

  a jobs
  b friends
  c work
  d money

5 Anna has three dogs. She takes _____ to the park every day. She loves her dogs.

  a them
  b it
  c they
  d him

6 My father has many books in his library. He has books about old cars and airplanes. He has _____ about gardening and cooking. He also has books on history.

  a papers
  b movies
  c books
  d magazines

7 Juanita is very shy. It is _____ for her to talk to new people. She doesn't like to go to big parties.

  a easy
  b difficult
  c friendly
  d fun

8 Chicago is a big city. It is called the "Windy City." It got that nickname, in part, because it is always _____ there.

  a cold
  b wind
  c windy
  d hot

Guess the Missing Phrase

Good readers think about what they are reading and guess what will come next. They get an idea about words before they see them. When they see the words, they can look at them quickly and then move on to the next sentence.

Practice 3

Write the phrase to complete each sentence.

on the weekend	be quiet	do the dishes	far away
close the door	go again	every time	get home

1 Louis and Cindy work hard during the week. They often work late into the night. However, _____ , they don't work at all. They relax and have fun.

2 The Wilson family had a great vacation last summer. They went to the beach and had a wonderful time. They want to _____ next year.

3 The traffic on Fridays is terrible. It can sometimes take up to two hours to _____ !

4 Tonya likes to do her homework with a partner. She doesn't like to go to the library because you can't socialize, and you have to _____ there.

5 The mountains are very _____ from the city. It takes five hours to get there by car.

6 Henry's sister is afraid of spiders. She screams _____ she sees one.

7 We all have jobs at our house. My father buys the food for the meals. My mother cooks. My sister cleans the kitchen, and I _____ .

8 It's cold! Please _____ and shut the window!

Practice 4

Circle the letter of the phrase that correctly completes the sentence.

1 Manuel usually eats the same food for breakfast. He eats eggs, bread, and fruit. Today, he doesn't want his usual breakfast. He just wants _____ .
   a some breakfast
   b some lunch
   c some coffee
   d eggs, bread, and fruit

2 I have two dogs. Their names are Salty and Pepper. They are very different from each other. Salty is white. Pepper is black. Salty is big. Pepper is small. Salty likes to play outside. Pepper likes to _____ .

   a stay indoors

   b eat a lot

   c bark at the television

   d drink water

3 The Munsatt family doesn't want to buy the house. The kitchen is very small and there are only two bedrooms. Also, the bathroom only has a shower. Mrs. Munsatt likes _____ .

   a eating in the dining room

   b taking baths

   c brushing her teeth

   d reading the newspaper

4 Mr. and Mrs. Nelson own a pizza restaurant at the beach. During the summer, the beach is very busy. They work every day. In the winter, there are not many people at the beach. It is very cold. Mr. and Mrs. Nelson _____ in the winter.

   a take a vacation

   b sell a lot of pizza

   c go swimming

   d are very busy

5 Claudia doesn't have a lot of money, but she likes to go shopping. She usually shops at the store on Pond Street. The prices are low there. She never shops at the stores on Main Street. They _____ .

   a have interesting things

   b are very cheap

   c have low prices

   d are very expensive

6 The children _____ the bus at 3:00. They walk home and have a snack. After their snack, they play outside. They like to ride their bicycles.

   a get off

   b get into

   c drive onto

   d play on

Practice 5

Write the phrase to complete each sentence.

listen to music	nice person	Russian students	do her homework
next year	drive safely	slept well	make more money

1 There is live music on Saturday evenings at the coffee shop. Many people like to go there to _____ .

2 Last week, Joe was sick. His neighbor brings him soup when he gets sick. She is a really _____ .

3 There are students from many countries in my class. There are students from China, Japan, and Argentina. There are also German and French students. There are no _____ .

4 Kira was too busy at work to take a vacation this year. She really needs a vacation, though. She is making plans to go _____ .

5 Heather is excited about her new job. She will have better hours and more interesting work. The most important part is that she will _____ .

6 Last week, Jeff had a bad cold. He coughed a lot, and it was difficult for him to breathe. Now he is feeling better. Last night, he _____ .

7 The mountain roads can be very dangerous. It is important to pay attention and _____ .

8 After dinner, Linda's friends are going to the movies. Linda isn't able to go, though. She has to _____ .

Thinking in English Practice Test

Write the phrase to complete each sentence.

Follow me	come here	next time	all day long
Don't worry	Excuse me	a few	
hurry up	Good job	Be careful	

1 He usually studies _____ .

2 Please take _____ oranges for your lunch.

3 _____ on your bicycle. The streets are dangerous.

4 Susan, please _____ . I want to see your dress.

5 _____ about the test. It's easy.

6 _____ , do you know where the bathroom is?

7 I heard that restaurant is good. Let's go there _____ .

8 I can show you the bathroom. _____ .

9 You made the best project in the class. _____ !

10 We are really late. Please _____ !

Dictionary Words

CHOOSING WORDS TO LEARN

Copyright © 2017 by Pearson Education, Inc. Duplication is not permitted.

> ### Presentation
> **Learning New Words**
> You will find many new words when you read. You can learn these new words and improve your reading skills and vocabulary. Follow these steps for learning new words:
>
> - Read the text to the end without stopping.
> - Read the text again. Underline the new words and write them beside the text or on a different piece of paper.
> - Find the new words in a dictionary. Write the parts of speech and the sentences with the words from the text.
> - Write the words in your vocabulary notebook. Write the parts of speech, the sample sentences, and the meanings of each word.
> - Practice reading and saying the new words aloud.

Practice 1

Read the text. Choose two new words from the text. Complete a chart for each new word. Include the following:

- Word
- Part of Speech
- Meaning
- Sample Sentence

Do you need a job? If you do, you will need a good resume. A resume is a document that lists your work experience. You write the details of your past jobs on a resume. These details include the dates you worked and the type of work you did. You send your resume to the company that has the job you want. Sending a resume is the first step in getting a job.

_____   _____

_____   _____

_____   _____

_____   _____

_____   _____

Practice 2

Read the text. Choose two new words from the text. Complete a chart for each new word. Include the following:

- Word
- Part of Speech
- Meaning
- Sample Sentence

Do you want to go to the top of the world? Mount Everest is 29,029 feet high and is considered the highest peak in the world. Mount Everest is a popular place to go for mountain climbers. It is a very difficult climb. The weather, the lack of oxygen, and the steep climb make Mount Everest one of the most dangerous mountains to climb.

_____   _____

_____   _____

_____   _____

_____   _____

Practice 3

Read the text. Choose two new words from the text. Complete a chart for each new word. Include the following:

- Word
- Part of Speech
- Meaning
- Sample Sentence

Do you notice the birds around you? Bird watching is a popular activity around the world. Some bird watchers just observe birds with their eyes, but others use binoculars and telescopes. Often, birds can be heard but not seen. Many bird watchers can identify a bird just by its song.

_____ _____

_____ _____

_____ _____

_____ _____

_____ _____

Presentation

Most Common Words

a	because	for	his	made	or	than	to	what
about	been	from	how	make	other	that	took	when
after	but	get	I	me	our	the	two	which
all	by	give	if	most	out	their	up	who
also	came	go	in	my	over	them	us	will
an	can	good	into	new	people	then	use	with
and	come	got	is	no	said	there	want	work
any	could	had	it	not	say	these	was	would
are	day	has	its	now	see	they	way	year
as	did	have	just	of	she	think	we	you
at	do	he	know	on	so	this	well	your
back	even	her	like	one	some	thought	went	
be	first	him	look	only	take	time	were	

Practice 4

Read the text. Underline all of the words that are on the Most Common Words list.

When you think of sharks, which shark do you think of? Many people think of the great white shark or the mako shark. The truth is that there are many kinds of sharks in the world. Some of them are very big, and some of them are very small. Some of them are aggressive, and some of them are very gentle. Great white sharks and mako sharks are very aggressive. Whale sharks and basking sharks are mostly harmless.

Sharks are carnivores and only eat meat. They live on a diet of fish and sea mammals. Dolphins and seals are their favorite food. Sharks even eat other sharks.

Don't get near a shark's mouth! Sharks have very strong teeth. Their teeth are in long rows. Over time, their teeth get ground down or fall out. The teeth in the back row come forward to fill the empty spots. A shark may use over 20,000 teeth in its lifetime!

Storing and Studying New Words

Practice 1

Vocabulary Notebooks

Learning new words helps improve your English. One way to help you learn new words is to have a vocabulary notebook. A vocabulary notebook is a notebook used only for new words. There are many ways to organize a vocabulary notebook. Follow these steps and look at the sample below:

- Draw a line down the middle of the page.
- Write the new word on the left side of the page.
- Next to the word, write its part of speech (noun, verb, adjective, adverb).
- Below the word, write a sample sentence with the word. If needed, write other sentences to make the meaning clear.
- Write the meaning of the word on the right side of the page.
- Check the pronunciation. Then read the word and the meanings aloud.

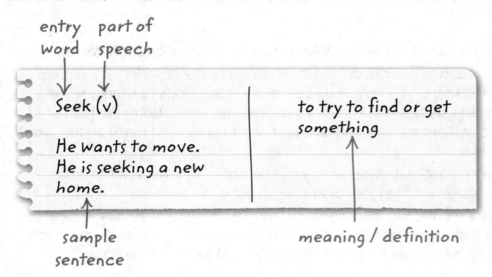

After you write the words in your vocabulary notebook, follow these tips for practicing the words on your own:

- Put your hand over the meanings. Read the words. Can you remember the meanings? Say them if you can. Review the words and meanings you don't remember.
- Write the words on a different piece of paper. Can you spell the words correctly? Practice the words you misspelled.
- Test yourself many times during the week.
- Write other sentences with the words.
- Look for the words in other readings.
- Try to use the words in conversation.

- Make study cards for each new word. (See sample below.)
- Look at the word cards every day.
- Play games with the words. (See ideas below.)

Study Cards

Study cards are made from small cards (3x5 inches/7x12 centimeters). Use the cards to study new words at home, on the bus, at the bus stop, in the car, waiting for class—wherever! Follow these instructions on how to make the cards:

- On one side of the card, write the word in big letters in the middle of the card.
- In the right corner of the card, write the word's part of speech.
- Below the word, write a sample sentence.
- On the back of the card, write the word's meaning. Draw a picture of the word or concept, if possible. Pictures can help you remember things easily.

Use your study cards to practice new words. Follow these tips for practicing the words on your own:

- Look at the cards. Say the word aloud and try to remember its meaning. If you don't remember the word, look at the meaning on the other side of the card. Put the words you don't know in a separate pile. Review those words again.

- Look at the meaning side of each card. Say and spell the words aloud. Check the spelling on the other side. Put the words you don't know in a separate pile. Review those words again.

- Practice your words with another student. Test each other by saying each word and asking for its meaning or by giving the meaning and asking for the word.

- Make new cards with a word on one card and its meaning on a different card (single-sided study cards). Play matching games, memory games, or categorizing games with the cards. (See ideas below.)

Study Card Games (Play with single-sided study cards.)

Matching Game: (can be played alone or with two or more players) Put all of the study cards face up on a table. Take turns matching the word cards to the definition cards.

Memory Game: (can be played alone or with two or more players) Put all the single-sided study cards face down on a table. Pick up two cards and see if they match (a word with the correct definition). If they don't match, put them back down on the table. Try again, or, if you are playing with a partner, take turns.

Go Fish: (for two or more players) Pass out five cards to each player (or fewer cards, depending on how many cards there are). Place the remaining cards face down in a pile in the middle. Take turns asking the other players if they have a match to the card you are looking for. If they have it, they have to give the card to the person who asked for it. If they don't have it, they say, "Go Fish," and the player picks a card from the pile in the middle.

Sad Jack: (for two or more players) One player picks a card and writes the number of spaces for each letter of the word. The other players guess the letters in the word. For each wrong letter, the player who knows the word draws a part of a face on the board (or on paper). Face parts can include head, eyes, nose, mouth, ears, hair, and so on. If a complete face is drawn before the word is guessed, then the player wins.

Password: (for two or more players or teams) One player describes a word to the other players without directly saying the word. The player who guesses the word first gets a point. The player/team with the most points in the end wins.

Practice 2

Read the text. Choose two new words from the text. Write them as you would in your vocabulary notebook, using this outline:

- Word
- Part of Speech
- Sample sentence
- Meaning / definition

It's important to have good study habits at home. There are many distractions at home, and it can be hard to study. Study in an area without a television or radio. These can be very distracting. Also, turn off your phone when you study. A phone call can take you away from your studies.

_____   _____

_____   _____

_____   _____

_____   _____

_____   _____

Practice 3

Read the text. Choose two new words from the text. Write them as you would in your vocabulary notebook, using this outline:

- Word
- Part of Speech
- Sample sentence
- Meaning / definition

We all know that classical music helps relax your body and mind, but many researchers agree that classical music also makes you smarter. There is something about the music that helps our brains focus. Many studies show that people are able to do mental tasks better and faster after listening to classical music. This is called the "Mozart Effect."

_____   _____

_____   _____

_____   _____

_____   _____

Practice 4

Read the text. Choose two new words from the text. Write them as you would in your vocabulary notebook, using this outline:

- Word
- Part of Speech
- Sample sentence
- Meaning / definition

One of the most amazing natural places in the world is the Grand Canyon. It is located in the state of Arizona, and many visitors go there each year to see natural beauty. Arizona is a dry state. The Yuma Desert is in Arizona. Many kinds of cacti and lizards live in the desert.

_____   _____

_____   _____

_____   _____

_____   _____

Practice 5

Read the text on the next page. Choose two new words from the text. Write information for both words as you would provide on study cards. Complete the information as outlined below.

Study Card (front)

- Part of Speech
- Word
- Sample sentence

Study Card (back)

• Meaning / definition

Many people practice martial arts. Karate, taekwondo, and judo are all forms of martial arts. People practice martial arts for various reasons. Exercise, self-defense, self-control, and competition are all reasons that people practice martial arts. Martial arts originated in Asia but are now very popular around the world.

_____   _____

_____   _____

_____   _____

_____   _____

Practice 6

Read the text. Choose two new words from the text. Write information for both words as you would provide on study cards. Complete the information as outlined below.

Study Card (front)

• Part of Speech
• Word
• Sample sentence

Study Card (back)

• Meaning / definition

There is little that is known for certain about Cleopatra, queen of the Nile. She was born in 69 BCE in Alexandria, Egypt. Cleopatra was the last pharaoh, or ruler, of ancient Egypt. Rome took control of Egypt after Cleopatra's death. People believe that Cleopatra killed herself after the suicide of her husband, Mark Antony.

_____   _____

_____   _____

_____   _____

_____   _____

_____   _____

Tips for Reading Tests

Presentation

Understanding Instructions

Reading tests are common in school. It is important to read the test instructions carefully so you know what to do. Follow these steps:

- Read the instructions.
- Reread the instructions if you don't understand them.
- Ask the teacher if you have any questions.

The following are common commands used in instructions. Learn the meaning of each one:

- Write the missing word.
- Underline the verb.
- Circle the noun.
- Match the word with the picture.
- Write in the missing letters.
- Answer the question.
- Interview your partner.
- Complete the sentence with a word from the reading.
- Add a suffix to the end of each word.
- Work with a partner.

Practice 1

Read the instructions. Then draw a line to match the instruction to the exercise.

1 Write the missing word in the sentence.

2 Underline the verb in the sentence.

3 Match the word with its meaning.

4 Write in the missing letter.

5 Answer the question.

6 Add a prefix to each word.

What is the title of this book?

h __ w

My brother always sweeps the floor.

____ view, ____ read

cafeteria: a restaurant where people serve themselves

They have three cats, two dogs, and a horse. They _____ animals very much.

Presentation

Previewing Questions

It is important to preview test questions before you read. As you read the text, look for answers to the questions. This will save you time.

- Read the questions.
- Read the text. Underline the sentences or words that answer a question.
- Answer the questions. For each question, go back and find the answer in the text.
- If you are not sure about an answer, reread the section of text again.
- Look over your test answers if there is time.

Practice 2

Read the story and answer the questions. Use the strategies for previewing questions from the Presentation on this page and on the last page.

The Last Theft

One day, a shop owner saw a man steal some food from his store. Before the man left the store, the owner caught him. The owner asked him why he had stolen the food. The man said that he needed it to feed his family. He said he had lost his job and had no money. As soon as the owner heard the story, he let him go with the food. Before the man left, however, the owner told him to come back the next day. The man returned, and the owner gave him a job. After he got the job, the man never stole again.

Questions

1. Why did the man steal the food?

2. Why does the man have no money?

3. What did the owner do to the man?

_____

_____

_____

_____

_____

_____

LANGUAGE IN CONTEXT

Practice 1

Part 1

Read the text. Underline the words in the paragraph that appear in the box.

my	at	and
on	our	had
went	with	over

My family goes on a summer vacation every year. Last summer, we went camping at a nearby lake. We brought our boat with us, and we relaxed and swam in the lake every day. Every night, we had a big campfire. We roasted hot dogs and marshmallows over the fire and sang songs. We had a great time.

Part 2

Read the text. Circle the correct answer.

My family goes on a summer vacation every year. Last summer, we went camping at a nearby lake. We brought our boat with us, and we relaxed and swam in the lake every day. Every night, we had a big campfire. We roasted hot dogs and marshmallows over the fire and sang songs. We had a great time.

1	The family goes on a winter vacation every year.	true	false
2	Last summer, the family went camping.	true	false
3	They hiked around the lake every day.	true	false
4	Every night, they played the guitar.	true	false
5	The family ate hot dogs.	true	false

Part 3

Read the text. Then read the sentence and circle the letter of the best meaning for the underlined word.

My family goes on a summer vacation every year. Last summer we went camping at a nearby lake. We brought our boat with us, and every day we relaxed and swam in the lake. Every night we had a big campfire. We roasted hotdogs and marshmallows over the fire and sang songs. We had a great time.

1 Last summer, we went camping at a <u>nearby</u> lake.
   a small
   b close
   c pretty
   d faraway

2 We brought our boat with us, and we <u>relaxed</u> and swam in the lake every day.
  a slept
  b read
  c rested
  d worked

3 We <u>roasted</u> hot dogs and marshmallows over the fire and sang songs.
  a ate
  b burned
  c cooked
  d baked

4 Last summer, we went <u>camping</u> at a nearby lake.
  a to hike
  b to sleep in a cabin
  c to walk
  d to sleep in a tent outside

5 We had a <u>great</u> time.
  a wonderful
  b OK
  c scary
  d terrible

Part 4

Read the text. Then complete each sentence with a word from the box. Write the correct word in the sentence.

My family goes on a summer vacation every year. Last summer we went camping at a nearby lake. We brought our boat with us, and every day we relaxed and swam in the lake. Every night we had a big campfire. We roasted hotdogs and marshmallows over the fire and sang songs. We had a great time.

great	roasted	vacation	campfire
family	relaxed	nearby	camping

1 We always go on _____ in September.
2 I was very tired yesterday. I _____ the whole day.
3 My neighbors go _____ every fall.
4 I have a big _____ . There are ten of us!
5 There is a park _____ . Let's go there and have lunch.
6 My teacher this year is _____ . I really like her.
7 We made a really big _____ . It was huge!
8 The children _____ their hot dogs over the fire.

Practice 2

Part 1

Read the text. Underline the words in the paragraph that appear in the box.

do	that	the	is
you	of	a	

Do you need a job? If you do, you will need a good resume. A resume is a document that lists your work experience. You write the details of your past jobs on a resume. The details include the dates you worked and the type of work you did. You send your resume to the company that has the job you want. Sending a resume is the first step in getting a job.

Part 2

Read the text. Then read each sentence and circle the correct answer.

Do you need a job? If you do, you will need a good resume. A resume is a document that lists your work experience. You write the details of your past jobs on a resume. The details include the dates you worked and the type of work you did. You send your resume to the company that has the job you want. Sending a resume is the first step in getting a job.

1 You do not need a resume to get a job.	true	false
2 A resume is a document that lists the classes you took in school.	true	false
3 Details about past jobs are on a resume.	true	false
4 Send your resume to your teachers.	true	false
5 A resume is the first step in getting a job.	true	false

Part 3

Read the text. Then read the sentence and circle the letter of the best meaning for the underlined word.

Do you need a job? If you do, you will need a good resume. A resume is a document that lists your work experience. You write the details of your past jobs on a resume. The details include the dates you worked and the type of work you did. You send your resume to the company that has the job you want. Sending a resume is the first step in getting a job.

1 A resume is a <u>document</u> that lists your work experience.
    a a book about jobs
    b a piece of writing that provides information
    c a magazine
    d a job

2 A resume is a document that lists your work <u>experience</u>.

   a problems

   b skills

   c feelings

   d friends

3 You write the <u>details</u> of your past jobs on a resume.

   a dates

   b names

   c sentences

   d facts

4 Sending a resume is the first <u>step</u> in getting a job.

   a part

   b ladder

   c stair

   d work

5 You send your resume to the <u>company</u> that has the job you want.

   a person that gives you a job

   b place that sells goods or services

   c school

   d teacher

Part 4

Read the text. Then complete each sentence with a word from the box. Write the correct word in each sentence.

Do you need a job? If you do, you will need a good resume. A resume is a document that lists your work experience. You write the details of your past jobs on a resume. The details include the dates you worked and the type of work you did. You send your resume to the company that has the job you want. Sending a resume is the first step in getting a job.

job	resume	experience
step	details	company

1 Please write the _____ of your past jobs on the resume.

2 I am looking for a job. I need to write my _____ .

3 My sister works for that _____ . She likes her job.

4 Tom does not have any money. He needs to get a _____ .

5 I got a lot of _____ from that job. I learned a lot.

6 First, you have to write a resume. The next _____ is to get an interview.

Practice 3

Part 1

Read the text. Underline the words in the paragraph that appear in the box.

at	go	made
after	into	then
any	it	was

I often go to the movie theater on Academy Street. It wasn't always a movie theater. At first, it was a concert hall. Many musicians played there a long time ago. Then the war started and there wasn't any money for concerts. The building was empty for many years. After the war, the owners made it into a shoe store. Then they got old and sold it. Next, it became a restaurant. It was a restaurant for thirty years. After the restaurant owners died, the town bought the building. They made it into a movie theater. Now, many people go there to see movies.

Part 2

Read the text. Then read each sentence and circle the correct answer.

I often go to the movie theater on Academy Street. It wasn't always a movie theater. At first, it was a concert hall. Many musicians played there a long time ago. Then the war started and there wasn't any money for concerts. The building was empty for many years. After the war, the owners made it into a shoe store. Then they got old and sold it. Next, it became a restaurant. It was a restaurant for thirty years. After the restaurant owners died, the town bought the building. They made it into a movie theater. Now, many people go there to see movies.

1	The building on Academy Street was always a movie theater.	true	false
2	The building was first a concert hall.	true	false
3	There was a lot of money for concerts during the war.	true	false
4	After the war, the building was a shoe store.	true	false
5	It was a restaurant for thirteen years.	true	false

Part 3

Read the text. Then read each sentence on the next page and circle the letter of the best meaning for the underlined word.

I often go to the movie theater on Academy Street. It wasn't always a movie theater. At first, it was a concert hall. Many musicians played there a long time ago. Then the war started and there wasn't any money for concerts. The building was empty for many years. After the war, the owners made it into a shoe store. Then they got old and sold it. Next, it became a restaurant. It was a restaurant for thirty years. After the restaurant owners died, the town bought the building. They made it into a movie theater. Now, many people go there to see movies.

1 At first, it was a <u>concert</u> hall.
   a a person who plays music
   b a musical performance
   c a sport
   d a game

2 Many <u>musicians</u> played there a long time ago.
   a people who play musical instruments
   b students
   c children
   d athletes

3 The building was <u>empty</u> for many years.
   a a lot of things inside
   b nothing inside
   c broken
   d busy

4 After the war, the <u>owners</u> made it into a shoe store.
   a people who buy something
   b people who borrow something
   c soldiers
   d workers

5 After the restaurant owners died, the town bought the <u>building</u>.
   a a place to put cars
   b an open field
   c a city street
   d a structure with walls and a roof

Part 4

Read the text. Then complete each sentence on the next page with a word from the box. Write the correct word in the sentence.

I often go to the movie theater on Academy Street. It wasn't always a movie theater. At first it was a concert hall. Many musicians played there a long time ago. Then the war started and there wasn't any money for concerts. The building was empty for many years. After the war, the owners made it into a shoe store. Then they got old and sold it. Next, it became a restaurant. It was a restaurant for thirty years. After the restaurant owners died, the town bought the building. They made it into a movie theater. Now, many people go there to see movies.

restaurant	movie theater	musician	building
owner	war	empty	concert

1 I only like to watch movies in a _____ .

2 My father is a _____ . He plays the guitar.

3 That _____ is really expensive, but the food is good.

4 The old _____ on my street is falling down.

5 The _____ was long and hard on the country. Many people died.

6 Do you know who the _____ of that restaurant is?

7 The _____ was great, but the music was too loud.

8 That building was a movie theater, but now it is _____ .

Practice 4

Part 1

Read the text. Underline the words in the paragraph that appear in the box.

her	out	they
like	so	up
or	their	were

The Anderson family was going on a camping trip. They were going to Bear Lake. The rain stopped the night before and it was a beautiful day. When they arrived, the girls got their bags out of the car and started putting up the tents. "The ground is so wet. I don't want to get my new shoes dirty," said Pamela. As Pamela stayed in the car, the other girls looked at one another. "Pamela doesn't do any work," said Julia. "I know! She never helps around the house," said Katie. "Either she doesn't want to get her clothes dirty, or she has to go inside and fix her hair," said Laura. Pamela wasn't like her sisters.

Part 2

Read the text. Then read each sentence on the next page and circle the correct answer.

"Everybody in the car! It's going to be dark soon," cried Mrs. Anderson. Julia, Katie, and Laura ran from behind the house and jumped in the car. Pamela walked slowly to the car. "We can't wait to get to the lake!" Julia and Katie screamed. "This is going to be so much fun!" cried Laura. Pamela gave a big sigh and didn't say anything

The Anderson family was going on a camping trip. They were going to Bear Lake. The rain had stopped the night before, and it was a beautiful day. When they arrived, the girls got their bags out of the car and started putting up the tents. "The ground is so wet. I don't want to get my new shoes dirty," said Pamela. As Pamela stayed in the car, the other girls looked at one another. "Pamela doesn't do any work," said Julia. "I know! She never helps around the house," said Katie. "Either she doesn't want to get her clothes dirty, or she has to go inside and fix her hair," said Laura. Pamela wasn't like her sisters.

1 The Anderson family went to Bear Lake in a car.	true	false
2 Julie, Katie, and Laura were excited about the camping trip.	true	false
3 It was raining on their trip.	true	false
4 When they arrived, the girls went swimming.	true	false
5 Pamela never helps out around the house.	true	false

Part 3

Read the text. Then read the sentence and circle the letter of the best meaning for the underlined word or phrase.

"Everybody in the car! It's going to be dark soon," cried Mrs. Anderson. Julia, Katie, and Laura ran from behind the house and jumped in the car. Pamela walked slowly to the car. "We can't wait to get to the lake!" Julia and Katie screamed. "This is going to be so much fun!" cried Laura. Pamela gave a big sigh and didn't say anything.

The Anderson family was going on a camping trip. They were going to Bear Lake. The rain had stopped the night before, and it was a beautiful day. When they arrived, the girls got their bags out of the car and started putting up the tents. "The ground is so wet. I don't want to get my new shoes dirty," said Pamela. As Pamela stayed in the car, the other girls looked at one another. "Pamela doesn't do any work," said Julia. "I know! She never helps around the house," said Katie. "Either she doesn't want to get her clothes dirty, or she has to go inside and fix her hair," said Laura. Pamela wasn't like her sisters.

1 Pamela gave a big <u>sigh</u> and didn't say anything.
  a a heavy breath
  b a big laugh
  c a cough
  d a smile

2 When they <u>arrived</u>, the girls got their bags out of the car and started putting up the tents.
  a stopped
  b drove
  c got to a place
  d left a place

3 When they arrived, the girls got their bags out of the car and started <u>putting up</u> the tents.
  a sleeping in
  b fixing
  c raising
  d finding

4 "Either she doesn't want to get her clothes dirty, or she has to go inside and <u>fix her hair</u>," said Laura.

    a cut hair

    b make hair pretty

    c color hair

    d wash hair

5 Pamela <u>wasn't like</u> her sisters.

    a to be jealous

    b to be similar

    c to not like someone

    d to be different

Part 4

Read the text. Then complete each sentence with a word from the box. Write the correct word in each sentence.

"Everybody in the car! It's going to be dark soon," cried Mrs. Anderson. Julia, Katie, and Laura ran from behind the house and jumped in the car. Pamela walked slowly to the car. "We can't wait to get to the lake!" Julia and Katie screamed. "This is going to be so much fun!" cried Laura. Pamela gave a big sigh and didn't say anything.

The Anderson family was going on a camping trip. They were going to Bear Lake. The rain had stopped the night before, and it was a beautiful day. When they arrived, the girls got their bags out of the car and started putting up the tents. "The ground is so wet. I don't want to get my new shoes dirty," said Pamela. As Pamela stayed in the car, the other girls looked at one another. "Pamela doesn't do any work," said Julia. "I know! She never helps around the house," said Katie. "Either she doesn't want to get her clothes dirty, or she has to go inside and fix her hair," said Laura. Pamela wasn't like her sisters.

dark	put up	sighs	arrive
like	fix her hair	tent	

1 The sun went down, and now it is very _____ .

2 What time does the train _____ ?

3 I don't want to sit next to Henry. He always _____ in class.

4 We are going camping this weekend. We will sleep in a _____ .

5 Can you help me _____ this picture on the wall?

6 I am _____ my mother. We both have brown hair and blue eyes.

7 My sister likes to _____ a lot. She is always in the bathroom.

APPENDICES

Appendix 1

Taking Notes: Identifying Key Ideas

It is important to identify the key ideas in a given reading. Follow these tips for finding the key ideas in a text:

- Before you read, think about why you are reading. Are you reading to get a general understanding of the topic? Are you reading for specific information?
- Remember your reason for reading, and then skim the text. Look for the key ideas.
- Read the text at normal speed. Find the main idea of each paragraph and highlight it.

Practice identifying key ideas using the following text.

My favorite holiday is Thanksgiving. It is an American holiday and is on the fourth Thursday of November. On Thanksgiving, families eat a big dinner together. They have turkey, corn, potatoes, and pumpkin pie. Thanksgiving is a time to give thanks for the people and things in your life.

Appendix 2

Underlining and Highlighting

It is important to identify the key ideas in a given reading. Follow these tips for finding the key ideas in a text:

- Before you read, think about why you are reading. Are you reading to get a general understanding of the topic? Are you reading for specific information?
- Remember your reason for reading, and then skim the text. Look for the key ideas.
- Read the text at normal speed. Find the main idea of each paragraph and highlight it.
- Review your highlighted areas.

Tips for highlighting:

- Do not highlight every word.
- Highlight only the main idea—not the details.
- Use different colors to indicate different things. For example, use yellow for main ideas, pink for details, and orange for questions.

Appendix 3

Copyright © 2017 by Pearson Education, Inc. Duplication is not permitted.

Reading Strategies

There are many things to think about when reading. Follow these strategies to help you understand what you read.

- Think about the Content: Before you read, ask yourself, "What do I know about this topic? What do I know about this type of reading?" This can help you understand the reading.

- Preview: Read the title and the headings, and then look at the pictures, if there are any. This will help you understand more about what you are about to read.

- Use Context Clues: As you read, you may find some unknown words. Read the sentences around an unknown word. This context can help you understand the meaning of the word.

Skimming and scanning are two more strategies that can help you when reading.

- Skim for General Information: Read the text quickly to get the main idea of the reading.

- Scan for Specific Information: Read the text quickly to look for specific dates or terms.

Practice these reading strategies using the following text.

A Husband for Daughter Mouse

A Chinese Folk Tale

Once, there was a mouse family that lived in a stone wall. When it was time for the daughter mouse to get married, the father mouse went out to look for a husband. He wanted the best husband for his daughter. First, he went to the sun, but the sun said that the cloud was better. The cloud can cover the sun. Then the mouse asked the cloud, but the cloud said that the wind was better. The wind can blow the cloud. Next, he went to the wind. The wind said that the wall was better. The wind can't move the wall. At last, he went to the wall. The wall said that the mouse was better. The mouse can dig holes in the wall. The next day, the daughter married a handsome mouse. They lived happily ever after.

Appendix 4

The Most Common Words

These words are the most common words in written English. About half of the words in any reading are on this list. It is important to recognize these words and know what they mean.

Most Common Words

a	because	for	his	made	or	than	to	what
about	been	from	how	make	other	that	took	when
after	but	get	I	me	our	the	two	which
all	by	give	if	most	out	their	up	who
also	came	go	in	my	over	them	us	will
an	can	good	into	new	people	then	use	with
and	come	got	is	no	said	there	want	work
any	could	had	it	not	say	these	was	would
are	day	has	its	now	see	they	way	year
as	did	have	just	of	she	think	we	you
at	do	he	know	on	so	this	well	your
back	even	her	like	one	some	thought	went	
be	first	him	look	only	take	time	were	

Appendix 5

Transitions for Time Order

Use time-order transitions to show the order of events in a narrative or the steps in a process.

Time-Order Words	Examples
first, second, third	(Narrative) **First**, boil the water. **Second**, add the pasta.
to begin, to start	(Process) **To begin**, pour water into the coffee maker.
next, then, after that, later, finally, last	**After that**, measure the coffee. **Finally**, pour some milk into the black coffee.

Appendix 6

Part 1 Comprehension Skills

Look at each item. Circle the letter of the correct answer.

1 The article above is about _____ .

   a students running in a race

   b students who don't have time to exercise

   c students learning how to ride bicycles

   d students eating too much junk food

Gift Giving around the World

Giving in Japan

2 The article on p. 151 is about _____ .

    a living in Japan

    b the types of gifts that are common in Japan

    c things to buy in Japan

    d the type of food that Japanese people like to eat

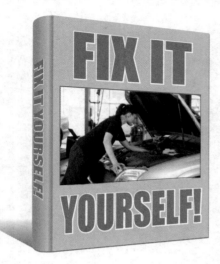

3 The book above is about _____ .

    a finding a good mechanic to fix your car

    b learning how to fix things around the house

    c learning how to drive

    d learning how to fix your own car

4 The book above is about _____ .

    a caring for your garden

    b planting a garden

    c taking care of indoor plants

    d staying indoors

Part 2   Comprehension Skills

Read the list. Check (✓) the topic of the list.

___ broccoli

___ carrot

___ celery

___ corn

___ lettuce

___ potato

___ radish

___ vegetables

Part 3   Comprehension Skills

Read the paragraph. Circle the letter of the correct answer.

I am never bored. I have so many hobbies that I don't have time to be bored! Some of my hobbies are things I do with my hands. I like to sew and knit. I also like to build things with wood. In addition to making things, I collect things. I have stamp collections and coin collections. All of my hobbies keep me busy!

1 The topic of this paragraph is _____ .

  a being bored

  b hobbies

  c making things

  d collecting

People in every country have different ways of greeting one another. People in France, Spain, and Italy greet people they know with kisses. They kiss both cheeks once. People in Japan and Korea greet one another by bowing their heads. In the United States and Canada, hugs are a common way to greet people they know.

2 The topic of this paragraph is _____ .

  a making friends

  b hugging people

  c different ways of greeting people

  d other countries

How do you get to work or school every day? Traffic in most U.S. cities is a big problem. There are so many cars and trucks on the roads. For some people, it can take hours to get home. Traffic causes many accidents and a lot of pollution. It is a good idea to take the bus or drive with someone else. With fewer cars on the road, the traffic will not be so bad.

3 The topic of this paragraph is _____ .

  a driving to work

  b driving with other people

  c pollution

  d traffic

Part 4 Comprehension Skills

Read the paragraph. Determine the order of each event. Then number the sentences in the correct order.

There are many things to think about when you take a trip to another country. First, you need to decide where you will go. After you make your decision, you need to get your passport. You cannot travel to another country without a passport. Next, you need to buy your ticket. After that, you want to learn about the country you will visit. Next, you should write down all of the places you want to visit within the country. After that, you need to buy things for your trip. Finally, you need to pack your bag. Be sure that everything will fit in your bag and that it is not too heavy!

__ Write down all of the places you want to visit.

__ Get your passport.

__ Decide where you will go.

__ Buy the things you need.

__ Learn about the country.

__ Pack your bag.

__ Buy your ticket.

Part 5 Comprehension Skills

Read the paragraph. How many examples related to the main idea are there? Circle the correct number of examples in the paragraph.

Our planet is in danger. There are many things that we can do to help Earth. For example, we can reuse things instead of throwing them away. There is so much garbage in our world, which is bad for our planet. Another thing we can do is recycle plastic bottles. Instead of throwing these bottles in the garbage, we can recycle them so they can be made into other things. In addition, we can stop throwing garbage in the oceans. All of these ideas can help make Earth a cleaner place to live.

1

2

3

4

Part 6 Comprehension Skills

Read the paragraph. Underline the sentences that have a sequence key word.

Last summer, I found a dog along the road. He had a broken leg and was really hurt. As soon as I saw him, I picked him up and took him to the animal hospital. They told me that he was really hurt and may not live. The next day, the dog was much better. He couldn't walk yet, though. After a few days, I was able to bring him home. I named him Lucky because he was a lucky dog. Now that he is my best friend, I think that I am the lucky one!

Part 7 Comprehension Skills

Read the text and question. Circle the letter of the correct answer.

A: Excuse me. Is there a coffee shop near here?

B: Yes. There is one on Main Street.

A: How do I get there?

B: Walk two blocks and then turn right on Main Street.

A: Great. Thank you!

1 Where are these people?
  a They are at their house.
  b They are in their cars.
  c They are on the street.
  d They are on a train.

When I was young, I always wanted a dog. My parents never let me have one, though. They said that dogs were dirty and a lot of work. Now I am older and know differently.

Last summer, I found a dog along the road. He had a broken leg and was really hurt. As soon as I saw him, I picked him up and took him to the animal hospital. They told me that he was really hurt and may not live. The next day, the dog was much better. He couldn't walk yet, though. After a few days, I was able to bring him home.

When I took him home, I decided to name him Lucky because he was a lucky dog. Now that he is my best friend, I think that I am the lucky one! I am very happy with Lucky.

2 Why does the man say that he is the lucky one?
  a He is lucky that he did not get hit by a car, too.
  b He is lucky to have the dog in his life.
  c He is lucky because he didn't have a dog when he was young.
  d He is lucky because he works in an animal hospital.

Part 8 Vocabulary Building

Read the dictionary entry. Classify the underlined parts. Circle the letters of the two correct answers.

convenient /cən'vinyent / *adjective*, 1) useful

a pronunciation

b part of speech

c meaning of word

d entry word

Part 9   Vocabulary Building

Look at the list of words. Circle the correct prefix and its meaning.

rename	remove	relive	remind

Prefix: un, dis, mis, pre, under, re, non

Meaning: under, not, wrong, before, again

Part 10   Vocabulary Building

Circle the letter of the correct answer.

Which suffix can be added to the root word *bright*?

a er

b al

c ful

d y

Part 11   Vocabulary Building

Draw a line to match each word with the correct part of speech.

1 careful   adverb

2 care   verb

3 carefully   adjective

Part 12   Vocabulary Building

Read the sentences. Circle the word that explains the underlined word.

John's shirt was <u>filthy</u>. His mom tried to wash it, but it was so dirty that the dirt wouldn't come out.

Part 13   Vocabulary Building

Read the sentences. What part of speech is the missing word? Circle the letter of the correct answer.

My dog is very fast. He can run around the _____ in fifteen seconds!

a verb

b noun

c adjective

d adverb

Part 14   Vocabulary Building

Read the sentences. What is the general meaning of the underlined word? Circle the letter of the correct answer.

Mary is doing very well in school. She gets good grades, and she interacts nicely with her friends. She talks and works well with many classmates.

a works well

b works together with other people

c gets good grades

d has many friends

Part 15   Vocabulary Building

Circle the letter of the phrase that correctly completes the sentence.

I will be late for the meeting. Please _____ and start without me.

a go out

b go ahead

c go after

Part 16   Thinking in English

Write the phrase that correctly completes the sentence.

pay attention	make a mess	get a job
get wet	take a break	

1 My younger sisters always come in my room and _____ . They never clean it up, and it makes me mad!

2 The soccer players _____ after the first part of the game. They rest and talk to the coach.

3 Don't forget to bring an umbrella today. It is going to rain, and you don't want to _____ .

4 The students listen well and always _____ in class.

5 Many students like to _____ during the summer. They make money for the next school year.

Part 17   Thinking in English

Read the sentence. Circle the letter of the best meaning for the underlined word.

1 She didn't like people to notice her.

   a like

   b sit next to

   c observe

   d hate

2 Sophie was the <u>opposite</u> of Janet.
    a the same
    b very different
    c friend
    d classmate

3 When the teacher gave Janet the lead part in the school play, everyone was <u>shocked</u>.
    a surprised
    b angry
    c happy
    d sad

4 She started to feel more <u>comfortable</u> speaking in front of others.
    a afraid
    b nervous
    c relaxed
    d rested

ANSWER KEY

PRE-TEST

Part 1 pp. 1–2

1. d, 2. a, 3. c, 4. a

Part 2 p. 2

classroom

Part 3 p. 3

1. c, 2. c, 3. a

Part 4 pp. 3–4

3, 1, 4, 7, 5, 2, 6

Part 5 p. 4

3

Part 6 p. 4

Last year, I went to a party at my friend's house.;

As soon as I met him, I knew he was different from other people I knew.;

The next day, he called me, and we went for a walk in the park.;

After a few more months, we got married!;

Now, we are living happily!

Part 7 pp. 4–5

1. b, 2. b

Part 8 p. 5

b, c

Part 9 p. 5

Prefix: dis

Meaning: not

Part 10 p. 6

d

Part 11 p. 6

1. adjective, 2. noun, 3. adverb

Part 12 p. 6

lift

Part 13 p. 6

c

Part 14 p. 6

b

Part 15 p. 6

a

Part 16 p. 7

1. sit down

2. wait for me

3. write it down

4. have a party

5. take a shower

Part 17 p. 7

1. b, 2. b, 3. a, 4. c

COMPREHENSION SKILLS

Previewing and Predicting

PREVIEWING

Practice 1 pp. 8–9

1. a, 2. b, 3. c, 4. c

Practice 2 pp. 10–11

1. b, 2. c, 3. b, 4. b

Practice 3 p. 12

1. a, 2. b, 3. c, 4. d

Practice 4 pp. 13–14

1. d, 2. c, 3. b, 4. a

PREDICTING

Practice 1 p. 15

1. a, 2. b, 3. c, 4. a

Practice 2 pp. 16–18

1. Ideas in the book: history of the holiday, description of the holiday, activities for celebrating the holiday, date of the holiday
   Ideas not in the book: flowers, cutting down trees, tree diseases

2. Information in the book: description of floating markets, location of floating markets, things sold at floating markets, how to get to floating markets

    Information not in the book: people of Thailand, recipes for Thai food, places to visit in Thailand, floating markets around the world

3. Ideas in the book: rules of the sport, countries where table tennis is played, history of table tennis

    Ideas not in the book: where to buy a table tennis ball, a story about a girl who has a magic table tennis ball, a schedule of table tennis events around the world

Practice 3 pp. 19–20

1. a, d, e
2. c, d, e
3. a, d, f, g

Identifying Topics and Main Ideas

IDENTIFYING THE TOPIC OF A LIST

Practice 1 p. 21

1. c, 2. f, 3. a, 4. c, 5. d

Practice 2 p. 21

1. family
2. classroom
3. computer
4. nature
5. sport
6. celebration

Practice 3 p. 22

1. meal
2. subject
3. symptom
4. money
5. drink
6. country

UNDERSTANDING PARAGRAPHS

Practice 1 pp. 22–23

1. b, 2. a, 3. b, 4. a, 5. a

Practice 2 pp. 23–24

a, c, d

IDENTIFYING THE TOPIC OF A PARAGRAPH

Practice 1 pp. 24–25

1. d, 2. c, 3. b, 4. d

Practice 2 pp. 25–26

1. d, 2. c, 3. b, 4. a

Practice 3 pp. 26–27

1. farmers' markets
2. birthday party
3. greenways
4. sushi

IDENTIFYING THE MAIN IDEA

Practice 1 pp. 27–28

1. d, 2. a, 3. c, 4. b, 5. b

Practice 2 pp. 28–30

1. b, 2. a, 3. d, 4. a, 5. d, 6. c

Practice 3 p. 30

1. The truth is that there are many kinds of sharks in the world.
2. Most sharks are carnivores and eat only meat.
3. Sharks have very strong teeth.
4. Sharks are very old.
5. There are many endangered sharks.
6. Sharks are endangered because people kill them.

Scanning

SCANNING FOR LETTERS AND LETTER COMBINATIONS

Practice 1 pp. 31–32

1. a, c, e, f, h
2. a, c, d, e, h
3. a, b, e, f, h
4. b, d, g, h
5. a, c, d, f, g
6. b, d, e, h
7. a, b, f, g
8. c, d, f, h

Practice 2 pp. 32–33

1. b, d, e, f, h
2. a, c, d, f, h
3. b, e, f, h
4. a, b, e, f
5. a, e, f, g
6. a, d, f, h
7. a, d, g, h
8. a, b, d, f, h

SCANNING FOR KEY WORDS AND PHRASES

Practice 1 pp. 33–34

1. a, c, f, h
2. d, f, h
3. b, d, g
4. a, d, g
5. b, d, f
6. a, e, h
7. c, d, f
8. a, e, h

Practice 2 p. 34

1. get out
2. turn on
3. clean up
4. pick up
5. save time
6. at night
7. across from
8. do over

Practice 3 p. 35

1. My favorite sport is lacrosse. Lacrosse is a team sport and was originally a Native American game. It is played with a stick and a ball. The stick **has** a net on it and is designed to catch and hold the lacrosse ball. Lacrosse is very popular in Canada and the United States.

2. Do you notice the birds around you? Bird watching is a popular activity around the world. Some bird watchers observe birds with their eyes, but others use binoculars and telescopes. Often, birds can be heard but not seen. Many bird watchers know which bird it is **just** by its song.

3. When we need something, we often go to the grocery store. However, a more interesting place to buy your food is at a farmers' market. Farmers' markets are all over the United States. Farmers **bring** their goods to the market to sell. Fruits and vegetables are not the only things for sale. Some farmers' markets have flowers, honey, and bread.

4. My family goes on a summer vacation every year. Last summer, we went camping at a nearby lake. We brought our boat with us, so every day we relaxed and swam in the lake. **Every night**, we had a big campfire. We roasted hot dogs and marshmallows over the fire and sang songs. We had a great time.

5. I am a member of a book club. A book club is for people who like to read and talk about books. My book club meets **once a month**. Other book clubs meet more often. Some book clubs read only fiction, and some read only nonfiction. My book club reads both kinds of books.

Practice 4 p. 36

1. I love flea markets. A flea market is a group of shops and booths. You can find almost anything from secondhand goods to crafts to food **in** a flea market. They are often only open on weekends. Flea markets began **in** rural areas, but now many cities **in** the United States have them, too. I go every year with my family. I like to look for unusual gifts there.

2. One of my favorite foods **is** sushi. Many people think that sushi **is** raw fish, but sushi **is** actually rice combined with vinegar and sugar. People like to put raw fish or vegetables on their sushi, though. Sushi **is** a nutritious and delicious meal!

3. Do **you** need a job? If **you** do, **you** will need a good resume. A resume is a document that lists your work experience. **You** write the details of your past jobs on a resume. The details include the dates **you** worked and the type of work **you** did. **You** send your resume to the company that has the job **you** want. Sending a resume is the first step in getting a job.

4. My great-grandparents were born in Germany. After **they** got married, **they** came to the United States in 1882. **They** wanted a better life. My great-grandfather worked as a baker, and my great-grandmother made dresses. **They** worked very hard and saved their money. **They** liked their new life in the United States.

5. It's important to have good **study** habits at home. There are many distractions at home, and it can be hard to **study**. **Study** in an area without a television or radio. Television and radio can be very distracting. Also, turn off your phone when you **study**. A phone call can take you away from your studies.

SCANNING FOR INFORMATION

Practice 1 p. 37
1. a, 2. c, 3. c, 4. c, 5. f

Practice 2 p. 38
1. b, 2. a, 3. c, 4. c, 5. b

Practice 3 p. 39
1. b, 2. c, 3. a, 4. c, 5. b

Practice 4 p. 40
1. a, 2. b, 3. b, 4. a, 5. a

Recognizing Patterns
RECOGNIZING TIME ORDER
Practice 1 pp. 41–42

1. a Think of a topic idea.
   b Research your topic.
   c Write your presentation.
   d Practice your presentation.
   e Give your presentation.

2. a Tom got sick.
   b Tom broke his finger.
   c Tom burned his foot.
   d Tom broke his arm.
   e School started.

3. a The mouse said, "Let me go."
   b The lion let the mouse go.
   c Hunters caught the lion in a net.
   d The mouse chewed through the net.
   e The lion and mouse became friends.

Practice 2
Part 1 p. 43
First : Turn right on Main Street.
Second: Go two miles and turn left on Market Street.
Third: Turn left on River Road.
Fourth: Go straight for four miles.
Fifth: Look for a park on your left.
Sixth: Turn left on Park Drive.
Seventh: Park your car in her driveway.
Part 2 p. 43
First: Pick up all of the papers.
Second: Throw the garbage out.
Third: Vacuum the floors.
Fourth: Clean the kitchen.
Fifth: Wash the dishes.
Sixth: Wash the stove and sink.
Seventh: Wash and dry clothes.
Eighth: Relax and begin the weekend.

Part 3 p. 44

First: Get an iron and an ironing board.
Second: Turn the iron on.
Third: Wait until the iron is hot.
Fourth: Put your shirt on the ironing board.
Fifth: Cover the wax spot with the paper bag.
Sixth: Move the iron over the paper bag.
Seventh: Continue until all the wax is gone.

Practice 3 pp. 44–46

1. a Michelle finished college.
   b Michelle moved to Tokyo.
   c She didn't like Tokyo.
   d She learned more Japanese and made Japanese friends.
   e She learned about the culture and enjoyed living in Tokyo.
   f Michelle left Tokyo to go home.

2. a The building was a concert hall.
   b The war started.
   c The building became a shoe store.
   d The building was a restaurant for thirty years.
   e The town bought the building.
   f The building became a movie theater.
   g People go there to watch movies.

3. a I was born in the United States.
   b My family moved to Spain.
   c I lived in Spain until I was five years old.
   d I lived in India for four years.
   e I lived in Mexico for five years.
   f I lived in Canada.
   g I live in California.

LISTING PATTERN

Practice 1 pp. 46–47

1. b, 2. c, 3. d, 4. c, 5. c

Practice 2 p. 48

1. For example, she is very kind.
   Also, she is very smart.

In addition to being smart, my grandmother is very humble.

2. For example, there is a great Chinese restaurant downtown.
   In addition to the Chinese restaurant, there is a little noodle shop near my house.
   Also, there is a nice French restaurant.
   Another favorite restaurant is the Brazilian steak house.

3. For example, it has a sun roof.
   Another good feature is the leather seats.
   Also, the seats have a heater!
   Other good parts about his car are the color, the speed, and the radio.

4. One of my most difficult classes is math.
   Another difficult class is World History.
   English, Social Studies, and Geography are all easy and fun.

5. One great thing to do is to go to the Statue of Liberty.
   Another great place to visit is Central Park.
   Also, the Broadway shows are fun to watch.
   Other good things about the city are the restaurants.
   In addition to the restaurants, the street vendors are also a great part of New York.

Practice 3 p. 49

1. For example, taking the bus is inexpensive.
   Also, you can get things done on a bus. You can read, work, or even sleep!
   Another reason to take the bus is the convenience.
   In addition, riding the bus can be fun.

2. One example is the schedule.
   Another example is the women's clothing.
   Another difference is how people greet one another.

SEQUENCE PATTERN

Practice 1 pp. 49–50

1. One day, I found a black cat in my yard.

   After the cat ate, it jumped in my lap and fell asleep.

   As soon as it woke up, it purred and drank some more milk.

   The next day, we saw a sign for a missing cat.

   As soon as the people saw the cat, they knew it was their lost cat.

   After they took the cat home, I was very sad.

2. Last week was my birthday.

   As soon as I got there, all of my friends jumped out from behind the couch.

   Before they gave me my presents, they sang "Happy Birthday" to me.

   After we ate, we played some music and had a dance party.

   The next day, I was tired but very happy!

3. When it was time for the daughter mouse to get married, the father mouse went out to look for a husband.

   Then the mouse asked the cloud, but the cloud said that the wind was better.

   Next, he went to the wind.

   At last, he went to the wall.

   The next day, the daughter married the handsome mouse.

Practice 2 pp. 50–52

1. a I found a black cat in my yard.
   b The cat ate.
   c The cat jumped in my lap and fell asleep.
   d The cat woke up and drank some milk.
   e I saw a sign for a missing cat.
   f The people saw the cat.
   g They knew it was their cat.
   h They took the cat home.

2. a It was my birthday.
   b I went to my friend's house for dinner.
   c All of my friends jumped out.
   d My friends sang "Happy Birthday."
   e My friends gave me presents.
   f We ate.
   g We had a dance party.
   h I was tired but happy.

3. a It was time for the daughter to marry.
   b The father mouse went to look for a husband.
   c The father went to the sun.
   d The father went to the cloud.
   e The father went to the wind.
   f The father went to the wall.
   g The daughter married a handsome mouse.

Practice 3

Part 1 pp. 52–53

First: A shop owner saw a man steal from his store.

Second: The owner caught the man.

Third: The owner listened to the man's story.

Fourth: The owner let the man go and told him to come back tomorrow.

Fifth: The man left the store.

Sixth: The man came back.

Seventh: The owner gave the man a job.

Part 2 p. 53

First: The grasshopper saw an ant.

Second: The grasshopper said, "Let's have some fun."

Third: The grasshopper said, "Winter is many months away."

Fourth: Winter came.

Fifth: The ant was happy in his warm house.

Sixth: The grasshopper asked for food.

Seventh: The ant said, "Next time, you need to prepare."

Part 3 p. 54

First: Tom bought a motorcycle.

Second: Tom took his motorcycle to a country road.

Third: Tom drove very fast.

Fourth: A police officer saw Tom.

Fifth: A police officer pulled Tom over to the side of the road.

Sixth: Tom went to the judge.

Seventh: The judge laughed.

Eighth: The judge gave Tom a speeding ticket.

Making Inferences

MAKING INFERENCES FROM PICTURES

Practice 1 pp. 55–56

1. c, 2. d, 3. a, 4. f, 5. d, 6. e

Practice 2 p. 57

1. a, 2. b, 3. d, 4. a

Practice 3 p. 58

1. d, 2. b, 3. c, 4. b

MAKING INFERENCES FROM RIDDLES

Practice 1 p. 59

1. b, 2. d, 3. a, 4. c, 5. d, 6. c

Practice 2 p. 60

1. pencil
2. whiteboard
3. paper
4. chair
5. table
6. eraser
7. book
8. computer
9. library
10. grocery store
11. park
12. restaurant
13. school
14. bank
15. bus stop
16. mall

MAKING INFERENCES FROM CONVERSATIONS AND STORIES

Practice 1 pp. 61–62

Conversation 1: 1. c, 2. b, 3. a, 4. c

Conversation 2: 1. b, 2. d, 3. a, 4. b

Practice 2 pp. 62–63

Conversation 1: 1. b, 2. a, 3. c

Conversation 2: 1. d, 2. b, 3. d

Practice 3 pp. 63–65

1. b, 2. c, 3. d, 4. a, 5. c, 6. b, 7. a, 8. c

Practice 4 pp. 65–66

1. "Everybody in the car!
   It's going to be dark soon," cried
   Mrs. Anderson.
2. Pamela walked slowly to the car.
   Pamela gave a big sigh and didn't say
   anything.
3. Julia, Katie, and Laura ran from behind
   the house and jumped in the car.
   "We can't wait to get to the lake," Julia
   and Katie screamed.
   "This is going to be so much fun!" cried
   Laura.
4. Pamela looked up.
   She looked all around her and then said,
   "Wait for me!
   I want to go with you!"
5. Julia laughed.
   "I just want her to help!"

Comprehension Skills Practice Test

Part 1 p. 67

1. b, 2. a

Part 2 pp. 68–69

1. a, 2. c, 3. c

Part 3 p. 69

1. b, 2. a, 3. b

Part 4 p. 70

1. a, 2. d, 3. b

Part 5 pp. 70–71

1. b, 2. c, 3. c

Part 6 pp. 72–73

1. b, 2. c, 3. a, 4. c, 5. b

Part 7 pp. 73–74

a You move into a new house.

b Look at each room and think what it is for.

c Ask yourself, "What will I do in each room?"

d Decide which pictures are best for each room.

e Decide where to hang the pictures.

f Hang the pictures on the walls.

Part 8 p. 74

1. b, 2. c

Part 9 p. 74

Last month, I got my driver's license!

Now I can drive anywhere I want to go.

Before I got my license, I had to take the bus to school.

One day, I waited an hour for the bus to come!

After that, I decided to study for my driver's test.

The next day, I signed up for the class.

As soon as I got my driver's license, I drove all around town.

Now I drive to school every day, and I never take the bus!

Part 10 p. 75

1. e, 2. b

Part 11 pp. 75–76

1. b, 2. b, 3. a, 4. c

Part 12 pp. 76–77

1. b, 2. c, 3. a, 4. a, 5. c, 6. b

VOCABULARY BUILDING

Dictionary Work

USING THE DICTIONARY

Practice 1 pp. 78–79

1. b, 2. d, 3. c, 4. a, 5. c, 6. d, 7. b, 8. a

Practice 2 pp. 79–80

1. a, 2. d, 3. c, 4. a, 5. d, 6. c, 7. a, 8. d

PARTS OF SPEECH

Practice 1 pp. 80–81

1. c, 2. b, 3. a, 4. d, 5. a, 6. b, 7. c, 8. b

Practice 2 p. 81

verb	adjective
weigh	boring
think	tiny
spell	beautiful
see	empty

adverb	noun
often	training
later	technology
slowly	information
carefully	director

FINDING THE RIGHT MEANING

Practice 1 pp. 82–83

1. b, 2. a, 3. b, 4. a, 5. b, 6. b, 7. a, 8. a

Practice 2 p. 83

1. (ceiling) fan, 2. (what) kind, 3. (my) trip, 4. (Americans) waste, 5. (can't) face, 6. (I) value, 7. (were) shocked, 8. (The) operation

Practice 3 p. 84

1. two, 2. who, 3. give, 4. make, 5. all, 6. they, 7. time, 8. what, 9. you, 10. were, 11. only, 12. into, 13. come, 14. and, 15. been, 16. can, 17. its, 18. look, 19. get, 20. how, 21. our, 22. use, 23. so, 24. from

Practice 4 p. 85

1. their, 2. day, 3. for, 4. would, 5. people,
6. thought, 7. made, 8. most, 9. think,
10. your, 11. could, 12. want, 13. was,
14. than, 15. there, 16. will, 17. year,
18. other, 19. because, 20. about,
21. said, 22. some, 23. when

Practice 5 p. 86

Practice 6 p. 87

1. **A:** Do you want to go to the movies
    tonight?
   B: I have to work tonight.
   A: How about tomorrow?
   B: That sounds good. What time?
   A: I think it begins at 9:00 P.M.

2. **A:** Are you ready for dinner?
   B: Not yet.
   A: I thought you would be hungry.
   B: I ate two sandwiches for lunch.

3. **A:** Excuse me, which building is the
    library?
   B: I think it's over there.
   A: Thank you. Also, are there any
    restaurants around here?
   B: What kind of food do you want?
   A: Any kind. I am very hungry.

Word Parts

PREFIXES

Practice 1 pp. 88–89

1. **Prefix:** un
   Meaning: not
2. **Prefix:** mis
   Meaning: wrong
3. **Prefix:** non
   Meaning: not
4. **Prefix:** dis
   Meaning: not
5. **Prefix:** pre
   Meaning: before
6. **Prefix:** re
   Meaning: again

Practice 2 p. 89

1. a, 2. a, 3. b, 4. b, 5. a, 6. a, 7. b, 8. a

Practice 3 p. 90

1. unhappy, unfriendly, uncomfortable,
   unnecessary
2. nonstop, nonsense, nonsmoker
3. preview, preorder, prepay
4. misunderstands, misuses, misspells

SUFFIXES

Practice 1 pp. 90–91

1. root: verb
   suffix: noun
2. root: adjective
   suffix: adverb
3. root: adjective
   suffix: noun
4. root: verb
   suffix: adjective
5. root: adjective
   suffix: adjective
6. root: noun
   suffix: adjective

Practice 2 pp. 91–92

1. b, 2. a, 3. a, 4. b, 5. b, 6. b, 7. b, 8. a

Practice 3 p. 92

1. b, 2. a, 3. d, 4. c, 5. c, 6. a, 7. d, 8. a

WORD FORMS AND FAMILIES

Practice 1 p. 93

1. a adjective
   b noun
   c adverb

2. a noun
   b adjective
   c adverb

3. a adverb
   b noun
   c verb

4. a verb
   b adjective
   c noun

5. a adjective
   b noun
   c adverb

6. a verb
   b noun
   c adverb

7. a verb
   b noun
   c adjective

8. a verb
   b adjective
   c adverb

Practice 2 p. 94

noun
1. reaction
2. creation
3. preference
4. success

5. information
6. invention
7. discovery

verb
1. succeed
2. react
3. invent
4. inform

5. prefer
6. create
7. discover

adjective
1. successful
2. inventive
3. preferable

4. informative
5. creative

Practice 3 p. 95

1. a, 2. b, 3. a, 4. b, 5. a, 6. b, 7. b, 8. a,
9. b, 10, a, 11. a, 12. b, 13. b, 14. a

Practice 4 p. 96

1. a, 2. b, 3. a, 4. a, 5. b, 6. a, 7. b, 8. b

Guessing Meaning from Context

WHAT IS CONTEXT?

Practice 1 p. 97

1. once a month
2. He bothers us
3. We laughed
4. relax
5. bad luck
6. difficult

Practice 2 pp. 97–98

1. b, 2. a, 3. b, 4. a, 5. c, 6. b, 7. a

GUESSING THE MEANING OF WORDS

Practice 1 pp. 98–99

1. b, 2. a, 3. c, 4. d, 5. b, 6. c, 7. d, 8. a

Practice 2 pp. 100–101

1. a, 2. c, 3. d, 4. a, 5. b, 6. d, 7. c, 8. b

Practice 3 p. 101

1. verb
2. noun
3. noun
4. verb

5. verb
6. adjective
7. noun
8. adjective

Practice 4 p. 102

1. like
2. hobby
3. boxes
4. follow

5. found
6. small
7. world
8. interesting

Practice 5 pp. 102–103

1. b, 2. a, 3. c, 4. d, 5. a, 6. a

Practice 6 pp. 103–104

1. b, 2. a, 3. c, 4. c, 5. b, 6. d

How Words Work Together

PHRASES

Practice 1 p. 105
1. a decide
   b call someone
   c be certain
   d try hard
   e put sheets on a bed

2. a put something in the place where it is usually kept
   b say something bad about someone or something
   c wait to do something
   d stop a fire from burning
   e wear something on your body
   f tolerate someone or something

3. a take someone on a date
   b remove something from your body
   c look or act like someone
   d take control
   e begin a new activity

Practice 2 pp. 106–107
1. a, 2. c, 3. d, 4. e, 5. f, 6. b, 7. d, 8. d

Practice 3 p. 108
1. a, 2. b, 3. a, 4. c, 5. a, 6. c

Practice 4 p. 109
1. get off
2. pick out
3. give up
4. cross out
5. drop off
6. cheer up
7. pass out
8. lies down
9. gets up
10. get over

Practice 5 pp. 109–110
1. a, 2. c, 3. a, 4. b, 5. b, 6. a, 7. c, 8. b

PARTS OF SENTENCES

Practice 1 p. 111
1. Yoko
2. She
3. roommate
4. They
5. students
6. family
7. They
8. tourists

Practice 2 p. 111
1. is
2. goes
3. is
4. speak
5. study
6. visits
7. travel
8. visit

PERSONAL PRONOUNS AND POSSESSIVE ADJECTIVES

Practice 1 p. 112
1. She, She, them
2. He, it, his
3. They, they, Their, them
4. her, She, It
5. It, its, I
6. your, it, She

Practice 2 p. 113
1. They, their, It, them
2. She, She, her, she, Her, her, she
3. His, He, He, its, it

Vocabulary Building Practice Test

Part 1 pp. 114–115
1. c, 2. d, 3. c, 4. a, 5. d, 6. c, 7. b, 8. a

Part 2 p. 115
1. (can) rest
2. (a play) play

Part 3 p. 115
1. **Prefix:** pre, **Meaning:** before
2. **Prefix:** un, **Meaning:** not
3. **Prefix:** dis, **Meaning:** not
4. **Prefix:** non, **Meaning:** not

Part 4 p. 116
1. b
2. b
3. b
4. b

Part 5 p. 116
1. a adjective
   b noun
   c adverb

2. a adjective
   b noun
   c adverb

Part 6 p. 116

1. made it bright and shiny
2. clothes
3. exciting
4. secretly looking

Part 7 p. 117

1. b, 2. a, 3. c, 4. d

Part 8 p. 117

1. a step onto a vehicle (bicycle, train, bus)
   b step into a vehicle (car)
   c like other people
   d take a vacation
   e wake up

2. a try to find something
   b be excited about something
   c be careful
   d check something
   e find information in a book
   f respect someone

Part 9 p. 118

1. make a mistake
2. put on
3. at night
4. in back of
5. do the dishes

Part 10 p. 118

1. It, He, it
2. Their, She
3. Our, He, us, him
4. They, their
5. My, We

THINKING IN ENGLISH

Thinking in English Practice

Practice 1 pp. 119–120

1. b, 2. d, 3. a, 4. c, 5. b, 6. a, 7. b, 8. d

Practice 2 pp. 120–121

1. c, 2. b, 3. a, 4. d, 5. a, 6. c, 7. b, 8. c

Practice 3 p. 122

1. on the weekend
2. go again
3. get home
4. be quiet
5. far away
6. every time
7. do the dishes
8. close the door

Practice 4 pp. 122–123

1. c, 2. a, 3. b, 4. a, 5. d, 6. a

Practice 5 p. 124

1. listen to music
2. nice person
3. Russian students
4. next year
5. make more money
6. slept well
7. drive safely
8. do her homework

Thinking in English Practice Test p. 125

1. all day long
2. a few
3. Be careful
4. come here
5. Don't worry
6. Excuse me
7. next time
8. Follow me
9. Good job
10. hurry up

STUDY SKILLS

Dictionary Words

CHOOSING WORDS TO LEARN

Practice 1 p. 126
Answers will vary.

Practice 2 p. 127
Answers will vary.

Practice 3 p. 128
Answers will vary.

Practice 4 p. 129
When, you, think, of, which, do, you, think, of, people, think, of, the, or, the, The, is, that, there, are, of, in, the, Some, of, them, are, and, some, of them, are, Some, of, them, are, and, some, of, them, are, and, are, and, are
are, and, only, They, on, a, of, and, and, are, their, even, other
get, a, have, Their, are, in, Over, their, get, or, out, The, in, the, back, come, to, the, A, use, over, in, its

Storing and Studying New Words

Practice 1 pp. 130–132
Answers will vary.

Practice 2 p. 133
Answers will vary.

Practice 3 p. 133
Answers will vary.

Practice 4 p. 134
Answers will vary.

Practice 5 pp. 134–135
Answers will vary.

Practice 6 p. 135
Answers will vary.

Tips for Reading Tests

Practice 1 p. 136
1. They have three cats, two dogs, and a horse. They _____ animals very much.
2. My brother always sweeps the floor.
3. cafeteria: a restaurant where people serve themselves
4. h __ w
5. What is the title of this book?
6. ___ view, ___ read

Practice 2 p. 137
1. he needed it to feed his family
2. he had lost his job
3. gave him a job

LANGUAGE IN CONTEXT

Practice 1

Part 1 p. 138
My, on, went, at, our, with, and, and, had, and, over, and, had

Part 2 p. 138
1. false, 2. true, 3. false, 4. false, 5. true

Part 3 pp. 138–139
1. b, 2. c, 3. c, 4. d, 5. a

Part 4 p. 139
1. vacation   5. nearby
2. relaxed   6. great
3. camping   7. campfire
4. family   8. roasted

Practice 2

Part 1 p. 140
Do, you, a, you, do, you, a, A, is, a, that, You, the, of, a, The, the, you, the, of, you, You, the, that, the, you, a, is, the, a

Part 2 p. 140
1. false, 2. false, 3. true, 4. false, 5. true

Part 3 pp. 140–141
1. b, 2. b, 3. d, 4. a, 5. b

Part 4 p. 141

1. details
2. resume
3. company
4. job
5. experience
6. step

Practice 3

Part 1 p. 142

go, It, At, it, was, Then, any, was, After, made, it, into, Then, it, it, It, was, After, made, it, into, go

Part 2 p. 142

1. false, 2. true, 3. false, 4. true, 5. false

Part 3 pp. 142–143

1. b, 2. a, 3. b, 4. a, 5. d

Part 4 pp. 143–144

1. movie theater
2. musician
3. restaurant
4. building
5. war
6. owner
7. concert
8. empty

Practice 4

Part 1 p. 144

They, were, they, their, out, up, so, her, or, her, like, her

Part 2 pp. 144–145

1. true, 2. true, 3. false, 4. false, 5. true

Part 3 pp. 145–146

1. a, 2. c, 3. c, 4. b, 5. d

Part 4 p. 146

1. dark
2. arrive
3. sighs
4. tent
5. put up
6. like
7. fix her hair

POST-TEST

Part 1 pp. 151–152

1. a, 2. b, 3. d, 4. c

Part 2 p. 153

vegetables

Part 3 p. 153

1. b, 2. c, 3. d

Part 4 p. 154

5, 2, 1, 6, 4, 7, 3

Part 5 p. 154

3

Part 6 p. 154

Last summer, I found a dog along the road.

As soon as I saw him, I picked him up and took him to the animal hospital.

The next day, the dog was much better.

After a few days, I was able to bring him home.

Now that he is my best friend, I think that I am the lucky one!

Part 7 p. 155

1. c, 2. b

Part 8 p. 155

a, b

Part 9 p. 156

Prefix: re

Meaning: again

Part 10 p. 156

a

Part 11 p. 156

1. adjective, 2. verb, 3. adverb

Part 12 p. 156

dirty

Part 13 p. 156

b

Part 14 p. 157

b

Part 15 p. 157

b

Part 16 p. 157

1. make a mess
2. take a break
3. get wet
4. pay attention
5. get a job

Part 17 pp. 157–158

1. c, 2. b, 3. a, 4. c